SOUTH FLORIDA TREES

A FIELD GUIDE

Bill Buckley

SOUTH FLORIDA TREES

A FIELD GUIDE

Bill Buckley

Summer Wind Publications

Foxboro, Massachusetts

South Florida Trees — A Field Guide
By Bill Buckley
Copyright © 2015 by Bill Buckley
Published by Summer Wind Publications
Foxboro, MA
All photographs are by the author
Cover photo of Sea Grape *(Coccoloba uvifera)*
Interior design by White Cottage Publishing Company,
www.whitecottagepublishing.com
Cover design by Lisa Hainline—Lionsgate Book Design,
www.lionsgatebookdesign.com

To contact the author or to order additional copies of this book, visit: http://www.southfloridatrees.org
Printed in the United States of America
For Worldwide Distribution
ISBN: 978-0-9906769-0-4

Dedicated to my family – Deborah, Jared, and Molly
– for your love, patience, and support.

Scarlet Bush

CONTENTS

Coconut Palm, Flamingo,
Everglades National Park

INTRODUCTION

Subtropical Florida has a tremendous diversity of trees. This flora includes a mix of native North American and native West Indian species, as well as non-native trees that have escaped from cultivation, that is, have become naturalized.

This field guide is for those who wish to identify the native tree species of south Florida, as well as several of the more common or important non-natives. Descriptive text is paired with color photographs of the key features of each tree - characteristics of leaf and twig, bark, flowers, fruits, habitat, and general growth form are all covered.

Leaf form is accented as the first feature to view when attempting an identification; flowers and fruits are also obviously useful features and the times of the year when they will typically be present are noted. The naturalist should first place the tree into one of the basic leaf form categories and view the pages of that section to find the specimen. Within each category the trees are grouped in alphabetical order by plant Family - this allows trees with similar characteristics to be more easily compared.

Botany has its own language, and it makes sense for those who would engage in tree identification to become conversant with its basic terminology. Although most technical terms have been left out, a glossary of the basic botanical terms used in this book is included and with a little practice their use becomes second nature.

Trees tend to be variable in form, for example, young trees may have different characteristics compared to more mature specimens, and a tree growing in the pinelands may have a different growth form than the same species growing in a hammock. Representative trees of each species are shown, and explanations of the differences between younger versus older specimens are included. Some trees may be easily identified by just a single notable feature - Sea Grape, for example, has large, rounded leaves - most trees, however, will require a bit more sleuthing, two or more characteristics will be needed for a positive identification, yet this is an aspect that makes the whole process so compelling and rewarding for the field naturalist.

Area Covered

The area covered in this guide includes the counties that lie south of Lake Okeechobee - Lee, Hendry, Palm Beach, Collier, Broward, Monroe, and Miami-Dade counties, and the guide will also be useful along the coasts, to at least as far north as Clearwater on the Gulf and Titusville on the Atlantic.

Tree Identification

Identifying trees is a skill like any other, practice and perseverance pays off. Here are just a few typical questions to ask when studying an unknown specimen:

If a pine, how many needles are in each fascicle and how long are the needles? How long are the cones?

If a palm, are the leaves palmate or pinnate? Does it have a crownshaft?

If a hardwood, are the leaves simple or compound and what shape are the leaves or leaflets? Are the leaves toothed or not? Are flowers or fruits present? Are there any noticeable characteristics of the bark or the overall growth form of the tree?

With a field guide, a notebook for recording observations, a small hand lens for the finer details, and a bit of patience, the intrepid naturalist will be well on the way to becoming an expert in tree study.

Non-native Tree Species in Florida

Non-native species, also called exotics or aliens, are those that have evolved in a different part of the world, often on a different continent, and have been transported to Florida, typically by the actions of people, whether intentional or not. Most non-natives do not do well in a new environment; their seeds may escape to the wild but they are not adapted to the amount of precipitation, soil characteristics, or presence of herbivorous animals. Some non-natives, however, can survive in a wild environment, and a subset of those that have naturalized may do so to a spectacular degree, out-competing and finally displacing natives. This latter group we call invasive species. Well known examples in south Florida include Melaleuca (*Melaleuca quinquenervia*), Brazilian Pepper (*Schinus terebinthifolius*), and Australian Pine (*Casuarina equisetifolia*).

The Florida Exotic Pest Plant Council (FEPPC) is a non-profit organization devoted to supporting "the management of invasive exotic plants in Florida's natural areas by providing a forum for the exchange of scientific, educational, and technical information." Pest plant lists, management plans, and other information are available at www.fleppc.org.

No matter where you live, consider planting native trees in your yard or garden. Once established they require little care and will reward with beautiful foliage, flowers and fruits, as well as the birds and butterflies they attract.

Taxonomy

The common names of trees vary by country, or even by region within a country, but there is only one scientific name, a Latin binomial bestowed by taxonomists. For example, Coconut Palm is known as *Cocos nucifera* worldwide. Nevertheless, the plant Family that a tree belongs to, and its scientific name, may change as new phylogenetic information about a species becomes available. The names used in this book are, to the best of my knowledge, those currently accepted.

The Origin of South Florida Trees

During the entire Pleistocene epoch, which began 2.5 million years ago and ended 12,000 years ago, glaciers alternately advanced and retreated several times, changing the location of the Florida coastline dramatically. Each advance caused sea levels to drop and the Florida peninsula increased in size. Each retreat caused sea levels to rise and much of the southern peninsula was covered by the ocean. Thus, south Florida is young from a geological perspective and the existing trees all originated from adjacent regions.

Temperate zone trees came south overland from the coastal plain of the Atlantic and the Gulf of Mexico. These trees include Hackberry *(Celtis laevigata)*, Carolina Ash *(Fraxinus caroliniana)*, Sweetbay Magnolia *(Magnolia virginiana)*, Southern Bayberry *(Myrica cerifera)*, Live Oak *(Quercus virginiana)*, Winged Sumac *(Rhus copallinum)*, Carolina Willow *(Salix caroliniana)*, and Bald Cypress *(Taxodium distichum)*, among others.

Tropical zone trees, mostly from the West Indies, came north over water, their seeds carried in the digestive tracts of birds, or stuck to the bird's feathers. Lighter seeds were transported directly by wind, and some plants, such as Red Mangrove *(Rhizophora mangle)* and Coconut Palm *(Cocos nucifera)*, have seeds which are carried by ocean currents. Trees which arrived from the tropics include Gumbo Limbo *(Bursera simaruba)*, Pigeon Plum *(Coccoloba diversifolia)*, Sea Grape *(Coccoloba uvifera)*, Guiana Plum *(Drypetes lateriflora)*, Milkbark *(Drypetes diversifolia)*, Poisonwood *(Metopium toxiferum)*, Paradise Tree *(Simarouba glauca)*, and Mahogany *(Swietenia mahagoni)*, as well as many others.

South Florida is also home to a bewildering number of non-native trees which have been imported by people for various uses, and some of these have naturalized. Many, such as Orchid Tree (*Bauhinia variegate*) and Royal Poinciana (*Delonix regia*), are ornamentals cultivated for their attractive foliage and flowers. Others, such as Mango (*Mangifera indica*) and Papaya (*Carica papaya*), are grown for their delicious fruits. Still others, such as Australian Pine (*Casuarina* spp.), were first brought to Florida for use as windbreaks along canals and developed shorelines.

South Florida's trees are diverse, indeed! The national parks and reserves, national wildlife refuges, state parks, and the many county natural areas of this subtropical region present the naturalist with nearly unlimited opportunities to identify and learn about this unique flora!

Sand Pine

CONIFERS

Conifers are gymnosperms, an ancient lineage of seed plants that first appeared about 300 million years ago at the end of the Carboniferous period. They have needle-like or scale-like leaves with a thick waxy cuticle designed to resist drought. Conifers do not require water for fertilization, a pollen grain produced by the male cone is delivered by wind to the female cone, another adaptation to a time when the continents were drier than they are today. South Florida conifers include three species of pine, two species of bald cypress, and a juniper.

Longleaf Pine (*Pinus palustris*) is a tall tree with an open crown that ranges over the southeast coastal plain from Florida west to Texas and north to Virginia. Although the tree itself is not an endangered species, most of the old growth stands were harvested in the late nineteenth and early twentieth century and replaced with faster growing Slash and Loblolly Pine. Since the Longleaf Pine community is home to a very diverse set of plants and animals, the loss of those old growth stands has had detrimental effects on those understory inhabitants, and several are listed as endangered.

Slash Pine (*Pinus elliottii)* is similar to Longleaf Pine in form, but with a reduced natural range, from Florida west to Louisiana and north to South Carolina, although it has been planted in Texas and Virginia. It is a fast growing tree with valuable wood and is favored by the lumber industry; it apparently grows well even on soil degraded by mining and has been used in reforestation efforts in other countries, including Australia and South Africa.

Sand Pine (Pinus clausa) is the only pine whose natural range is mostly limited to Florida. It is a relatively short-lived tree that prefers dry, sandy soils in association with scrub oaks and other characteristic understory plants.

Bald Cypress (*Taxodium distichum*) is an impressively large tree that is in the same plant family as the Redwoods and Giant Sequoias of California. There is an old growth stand of Bald Cypress in the Audubon Society's Corkscrew Swamp Sanctuary, some of the trees are over 500 years old! The closely related **Pond Cypress (*Taxodium ascendens*)** is a smaller tree that is also found in wet habitats throughout Florida.

Southern Red Cedar (*Juniperus silicicola*) is a small evergreen tree with dense foliage and a pyramidal or spire-like shape. It grows well in a variety of habitats and tends to prefer limestone soils.

Australian Pine (*Casuarina equisetifolia*) is not a conifer; it is a flowering plant that is mentioned here because of its resemblance to pine trees. What look like pine needles are actually the photosynthetic twigs of the tree.

Southern Red Cedar
Juniperus silicicola

Plant Family: Cupressaceae

Leaves: Small and scaly on older growth, overlapping and hugging the twigs, dark green; short and needle-like on younger growth, bright green.

Bark: Gray to reddish brown, peeling in long strips.

Cones: Dioecious, female cones grayish blue, waxy, small, only 5 mm in diameter; male cones golden brown; present fall to winter and may stay on the tree for several months.

Habitat: Varied; this native pioneer species may be found in wet or dry habitats, including hammock edges, abandoned fields, coastal thickets, and disturbed sites.

Growth Form: Small to medium-sized densely branched tree with a pyramidal form.

Similar Species: The closely related Eastern Red Cedar (*Juniperus virginiana*) is found in northern Florida and has slightly larger cones. Some authorities consider Southern Red Cedar and Eastern Red Cedar to be varieties of the same species.

Comments: The common name is a misnomer as this tree is a juniper; it is not in genus *Cedrus*, which are the true cedars, large trees that inhabit mountains of the Mediterranean region, with one species found in the Himalayas.

Pond Cypress
Taxodium ascendens

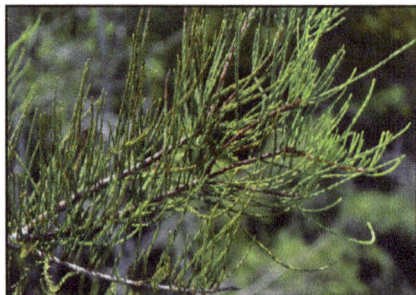

Plant Family: Cupressaceae

Leaves: Short needles, usually pressed against the twigs; on some branches the needles may spread out from the twigs to a greater degree; the needles are shed in the fall, though new growth may persist until winter.

Bark: Gray, furrowed, flaking off in strips, the branches are brown, the twigs often held upright along the branches.

Cones: A round green cone, to 3 cm, turning brown at maturity; typically seen summer to fall, but also at other times of the year.

Habitat: Wet areas with standing water.

Growth Form: Medium-sized to large tree with the base often thick and buttressed.

Similar Species: Bald Cypress (*Taxodium distichum*) is a larger tree when mature, has longer needles that are spread out from the twig, and is more likely to possess cypress knees, woody projections around the tree that rise from the roots.

Comments: Pond Cypress forms the circular dwarf cypress domes of the Everglades; it is found throughout Florida, west along the coastal plain to Louisiana and north to the Carolinas. Some taxonomists consider Bald Cypress and Pond Cypress to be varieties of the same species.

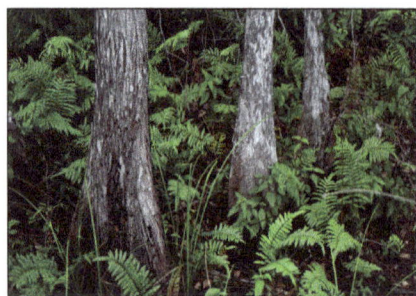

Bald Cypress
Taxodium distichum

Plant Family: Cupressaceae

Leaves: Short flat needles, usually spread out in two ranks from the twigs; on some branches the needles may be pressed against the twigs to some degree. The needles are shed in the fall.

Bark: Gray to brown, smooth, lightly fissured on older trees, the trunk is usually buttressed at the base and the branches are brown.

Cones: A round green cone, to 3 cm, turning brown at maturity; all year.

Habitat: Swamps, stream borders, and wet habitats with slow moving water.

Growth Form: A large tree with a thick buttressed base. Knob-like root growths called cypress knees may be present in deeper water.

Similar Species: Pond Cypress (*Taxodium ascendens*) has leaves with the needles usually pressed against the twig, is found in standing water, and is less likely to possess cypress knees.

Comments: Bald Cypress are tall, stately trees related to the Redwoods and Sequoias of California. They are found throughout Florida and in the lowlands of the southern States and also inhabit the Mississippi watershed as far north as southern Illinois. Some taxonomists consider Bald Cypress and Pond Cypress to be varieties of the same species.

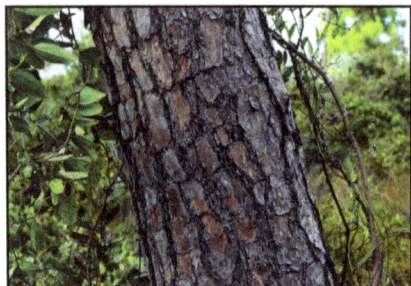

Sand Pine
Pinus clausa

Plant Family: Pinaceae

Leaves: Needles are in bundles of 2 and rather short, from 5 – 8 cm long, the leaf buds are brown.

Bark: Gray-brown, smooth on younger trees, having scaly orange and gray plates on older trees.

Cones: Short, to only 8 cm, when ripe they open to reveal two-toned scales, brown with a black band along the tip. They may persist on the tree for more than one year.

Habitat: Dry, sandy soils, often in association with scrub oaks, saw palmetto and prickly pear cactus, a community that ecologists refer to as sand pine scrub, most of which has been lost to development in South Florida.

Growth Form: Small to medium-sized tree.

Key Features: The two-toned scales of the mature female cones combined with smooth twigs are diagnostic.

Comments: Sand Pine will be found on poor, sandy soils from Collier and Broward counties north to the panhandle; it is a true Florida native.

Slash Pine
Pinus elliottii

Plant Family: Pinaceae
Leaves: Needles are in bundles of 2 (occasionally 3), 8 – 15 cm long, the leaf buds are green to light brown.
Bark: Gray-brown, flaky, with orange under-bark; fire scars may be present on the lower trunk.
Cones: The cones are usually less than 15 cm long and each scale is tipped with a short spine; present all year.
Habitat: Pine flatwoods, moist soils.
Growth Form: Medium-sized to a potentially large tree, but most of the older trees, to 30 meters tall have been logged.
Similar Species: Longleaf Pine (*Pinus palustris*) has cones greater than 15 cm long, silver-white buds, and in south Florida is restricted to Lee County.
Comments: Slash Pine is common in south Florida and forms the pine-lands of the Everglades; it is a tall tree that is fire dependent, having evolved cones that open when exposed to heat, generating new seedlings after a fire. The common name comes from the former practice of slashing the trunk to start the flow of the resinous sap, which was harvested to produce turpentine. Older trees may still be found with the scars that resulted from this practice.

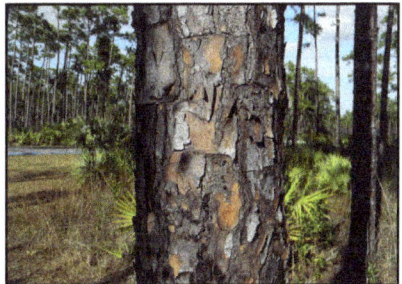

7

Longleaf Pine
Pinus palustris

Plant Family: Pinaceae

Leaves: Needles are in bundles of 3, 15 – 30 cm long, the leaf buds are whitish.

Bark: Gray and red-brown, flaky, fire scars may be present on the lower trunk.

Cones: The cones are usually greater than 15 cm long and each scale is tipped with a short spine; present all year

Habitat: Pinelands, often in pure stands, and having a very diverse understory of herbaceous plants. It is not common in south Florida, being restricted to Lee County.

Growth Form: Medium-sized to large tree.

Similar Species: Slash Pine (*Pinus elliottii*) has cones less than 15 cm long, brown buds, and is found in all the south Florida counties.

Comments: Longleaf pine is highly fire resistant in all growth stages. New seedlings look like tall clumps of grass; if subjected to fire the ends of the needles burn off but the central bud is protected. After a few years of root development the tree begins a fast upward growth spurt and is soon out of the reach of ground fires. Longleaf Pine forests once covered much of the southeastern U.S. but heavy logging and subsequent suppression of fires have reduced it to less than 3% of its former range.

Flowering Monocots - Palms

Flowering plants are called angiosperms, which first appeared roughly 140 million years ago in the early Cretaceous period and are today the dominant plants on earth. Angiosperms, unlike the gymnosperms, enclose their seeds within fruits.

Palms belong to one of the major angiosperm groups called the monocots, named for the characteristic of the seedlings having a single seed leaf. The monocots also include orchids, lilies, and grasses. Palms are the only monocots that take an arboreal, or tree-like form, although they mostly grow in height, very little in width, resulting in the tall narrow trunk that we associate with the palms. The entire trunk is composed of sapwood, palms lack the inner heart wood characteristic of many hardwood trees. The fruits of most south Florida palms are rounded drupes held in clusters, the major exception being the large three-sided husks of the Coconut Palm.

When attempting to identify a palm, it helps to initially note whether the tree has palmate leaves, such as Saw Palmetto, or pinnate leaves, such as Coconut Palm.

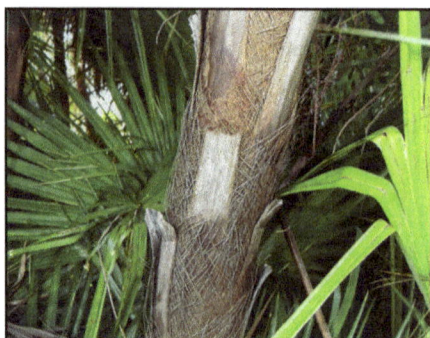

Paurotis Palm
Acoelorrhaphe wrightii

Plant Family: Palmae

Leaves: Palmate, green on both top and bottom, to 60 cm, the very long petioles have sharp yellow teeth.

Bark: Brown, heavily matted with old leaf bases.

Flowers: Yellow, held on stalks that are about 1 m long; appearing spring to summer.

Fruits: Round, orange, turning black when ripe, to 1 cm in diameter; mostly fall to winter.

Habitat: Hammock edges of the Everglades, also in landscaping.

Growth Form: A fairly small tree that always grows in clumps, with several narrow trunks presenting from the same rootstock.

Key Features: The palmate leaves with very long petioles, matted trunk, and clumping growth form, make this one of the easier palms to identify.

Comments: Paurotis Palm is considered threatened in the wild but it is widely planted as an ornamental.

Fishtail Palms
Caryota spp.

Plant Family: Palmae

Leaves: Palmate, but twice-compound, unlike all other palm species. The leaflets on each segment are shaped like the tail of a fish.

Bark: The trunks may be solitary or multiple, depending on the species, and are often covered with dark matting and old leaf bases.

Flowers: Small, white, in long, drooping clusters in the spring.

Fruits: Rounded, green, ripening to black, from 1 to 2 cm, depending on the species, typically held in long drooping clusters in summer to fall.

Habitat: Planted throughout south Florida, Fishtail Palms may naturalize.

Growth Form: Small to medium-sized trees.

Key Feature: The compound leaves with the distinctive leaflet shape are unique, allowing placement of any particular specimen of Fishtail Palm within the genus *Caryota*.

Comments: The Fishtail Palms are native to Asia and the East Indies and comprise as many as twelve species, several of which are grown in south Florida.

11

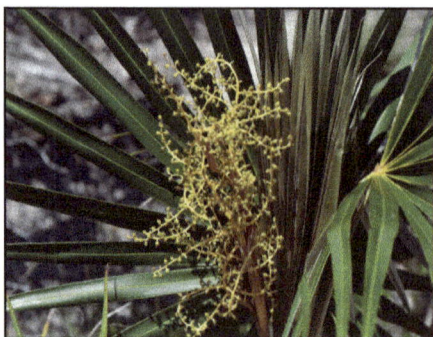

Silver Palm
Coccothrinax argentata

Plant Family: Palmae

Leaves: Palmate, to 1 m, divided for almost the entire length of the segments, petioles without spines, lustrous dark green above, distinctly silver beneath. The petiole, and its point of attachment with the leaf, is obviously yellow.

Bark: Light gray, fairly smooth, the rings are not obvious.

Flowers: Small, yellow, in upright clusters in spring to summer.

Fruits: Rounded, blue-black, to about 1 cm, in clusters, edible and sought by birds; reportedly made into a wine; seen summer to fall.

Habitat: Sandy coastal soils and pinelands, uncommon.

Growth Form: Small to medium-sized tree.

Key Feature: The lustrous dark green leaves that are distinctly silver beneath will separate Silver Palm from other palmate leaved species.

Comments: Silver Palm is listed as a threatened species in Florida, it can be seen on Big Pine Key and in Bahia Honda State Park, where there is a trail named after it.

Coconut Palm
Cocos nucifera

Plant Family: Palmae

Leaves: Pinnate, very long, to 6 m, the segments are held in two ranks off the rachis, in a single plane.

Bark: Gray, ringed; the trunk is often curved and it always lacks a crownshaft.

Flowers: Rounded, yellow, held in long clusters throughout the year.

Fruits: The familiar coconut, green, turning brown when ripe, a large three-sided husk that encloses the round seed or nut, one of the largest seeds produced in the Plant Kingdom.

Habitat: Beaches; widely planted; tolerant of a wide variety of soil types.

Growth Form: Medium-sized to potentially large tree.

Similar Species: Unlikely to be confused with any other palm tree.

Comments: The fruit floats and retains the ability to germinate even after many months in salt water, resulting in a worldwide distribution on tropical coasts. It has been called one of the most useful plants on earth - the fruits have many medicinal and culinary uses, the leaves are used as roofing for tropical dwellings, and the wood as building material and fuel in the tropics.

Key Thatch Palm
Leucothrinax morrisii

Plant Family: Palmae

Leaves: Palmate, over 1 m long, divided for only half the length of the segments, petioles without spines, green above, grayish-white beneath.

Bark: Gray

Flowers: White, fragrant, in drooping clusters, appearing in spring.

Fruits: Rounded, green, turning white, without stalks, to 1 cm in diameter; mostly summer to fall.

Habitat: Hammock edges, pinelands, sandy soils of the Keys.

Growth Form: Shrub to small tree.

Similar Species: Florida Thatch Palm *(Thrinax radiata)* has light green leaf undersides; Silver Palm *(Coccothrinax argentata)* has leaf segments more deeply divided; Cabbage Palm *(Sabal palmetto)* has a V-shaped leaf.

Comments: Key Thatch Palm is considered an endangered species and is probably most common in the wild on Big Pine Key; it is planted at other Key locales.

Date Palms
Phoenix spp.

Plant Family: Palmae
Leaves: Pinnate, green, very long, to 6 m, the segments are held in two ranks off the midrib, in a single plane. Lower segments take the form of sharp spines. Older, dead leaves hang off the top of the trunk.
Bark: Very rough, covered with old leaf bases in a helical pattern, the trunk is usually single, is widest at the base, and lacks a crown shaft.
Flowers: Yellow-white, in clusters that are 1 m long; summer.
Fruits: Orange-red, edible, to 2 cm in diameter; fall to winter.
Habitat: Planted throughout south Florida as beautiful ornamentals.
Growth Form: Medium-sized tree.
Similar Species: There are at least six *Phoenix* species in south Florida, and they are known to hybridize, so exact identification is difficult. As a group they are identified by the trunk covered in old leaf bases, the sharp spines on the lower leaves, and no crownshaft.
Comments: The Date Palms are native to Asia and Africa and are planted as ornamentals in Florida. They do not produce fruit here as well as they do in their native habitat.

Royal Palm
Roystonea regia

Plant Family: Palmae

Leaves: Pinnate, up to 4 m long, the segments are held in several planes off the rachis.

Bark: Light gray, the bulging trunk is cement-like and topped with a distinctive green crownshaft that may be 1.5 to 2 meters long.

Flowers: White, fragrant, in long drooping clusters, seen spring to summer.

Fruits: Rounded, green, ripening to blue, to 1 cm, in heavy drooping clusters; summer to fall.

Habitat: Hammocks; also widely planted along streets and highways in south Florida.

Growth Form: Royal Palm is a stately tree that is the tallest of Florida's palm species, rising to over 30 m.

Similar Species: Manila Palm *(Veitchia merrillii)* also has a green crownshaft, but has shorter leaves, a ringed trunk, and is smaller when mature.

Comments: The natural range of Royal Palm includes south Florida, Mexico, parts of Central America, the Bahamas, and Cuba, where it is the national tree. It is also planted in many other tropical countries as an ornamental.

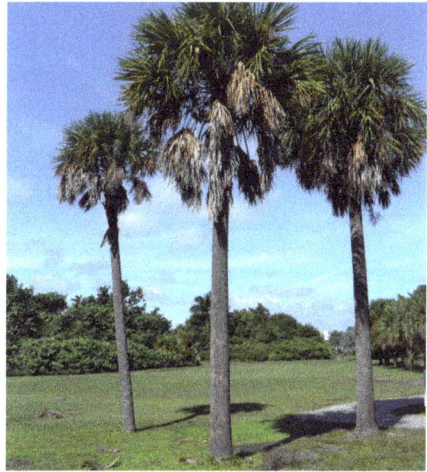

Sabal Palm
(Cabbage Palm)
Sabal palmetto

Plant Family: Palmae

Leaves: Palmate, the leafstalk extends well into the leaf, producing an obvious V-shape, green above, lighter green below, loose fibers are present.

Bark: Brown-gray, the trunk is sometimes prostrate on the ground, but is usually upright; in young specimens the trunk may be criss-crossed with old leafstalks, older trees typically shed the leafstalks.

Flowers: White, fragrant, in loose drooping clusters in the spring.

Fruits: Rounded, green ripening to black, to 1 cm, in clusters; summer to fall.

Habitat: Common throughout Florida along canals, in sandy soils, and in other habitats.

Growth Form: Shrub to medium-sized tree.

Key Features: The V-shaped leaf is unique and is the key feature regardless of growth form; the loose leaf fibers are also diagnostic.

Comments: Sabal Palm is the state tree of Florida, found throughout the Sunshine state.

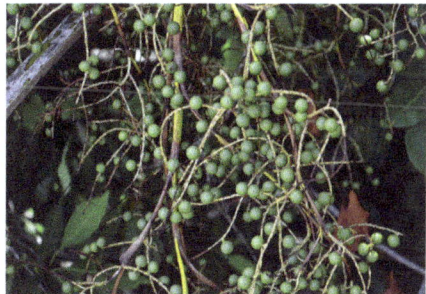

Saw Palmetto
Serenoa repens

Plant Family: Palmae

Leaves: Palmate, light green, the segments are divided for most of their length, the petiole is saw-toothed with many small but sharp spines.

Bark: The trunk is often prostrate on the ground or it may be upright; old leaf bases often cover the trunk.

Flowers: Small, white, held in long linear clusters in the spring.

Fruits: Rounded, blue-black, from 1 to 2 cm; summer to fall.

Habitat: Saw Palmetto is probably Florida's most common native palm, it is found throughout the state on sandy soils and in the understory of pine forests.

Growth Form: Saw Palmetto is often found in the pinelands as a shrub growing from a prostrate trunk, but in more open situations, such as along canals, or in hammocks, it may attain small tree status.

Key Feature: The saw-toothed petioles distinguish it from Sabal Palm. One does not walk through a Saw Palmetto understory wearing shorts!

Comments: Extracts from the fruits of Saw Palmetto are used to treat prostate disorders, although the effectiveness of such use is under debate in the medical community.

Queen Palm
Syagrus romanzoffiana

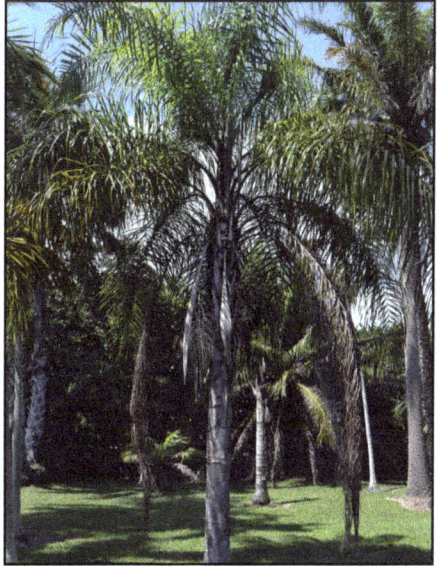

Plant Family: Palmae
Leaves: Pinnate, dark green, to 5 m long, the segments are held in more than one plane.
Bark: Light gray, smooth, ring scars rougher, sometimes old leaf bases will remain on the trunk; lacks a crownshaft.
Flowers: Whitish yellow, in large drooping clusters; spring to summer.
Fruits: Orange-red, edible, to 3 cm, in heavy clusters; summer to fall.
Habitat: Widely planted as an ornamental for its attractive form, this South American species has escaped from cultivation and is considered an invasive species in Florida, often appearing in hammock edges and along roadsides.
Growth Form: Medium-sized tree with long arching leaves.
Similar Species: The growth form resembles Coconut Palm (*Cocos nucifera*), but Queen Palm has leaves with the segments in more than one plane, and has orange-red fruits.
Comments: Older taxonomic references have Queen Palm as *Cocos plumosa* or *Arecastrum romanzoffianum*.

Florida Thatch Palm
Thrinax radiata

Plant Family: Palmae
Leaves: Palmate, over 1 m long, light green beneath, divided for only half the length of the segments, petioles without spines.
Bark: Has a slender gray trunk.
Flowers: White, fragrant, in hanging clusters in the spring.
Fruits: Rounded, white, short-stalked, to 1 cm, in long clusters; summer to fall.
Habitat: Coastal hammocks, sandy soil.
Growth Form: Shrub to small tree.
Similar Species: Key Thatch Palm *(Leucothrinax morrisii)* and Silver Palm *(Coccothrinax argentata)* have gray-white leaf undersides; Cabbage Palm *(Sabal palmetto)* has a V-shaped leaf.
Comments: Florida Thatch Palm is an endangered species, found in the wild in the extreme southern peninsula and in Keys hammocks. It is more common in the West Indies, and on the coasts of Mexico and Central America.

20

Manila Palm
(Christmas Palm)
Veitchia merrillii

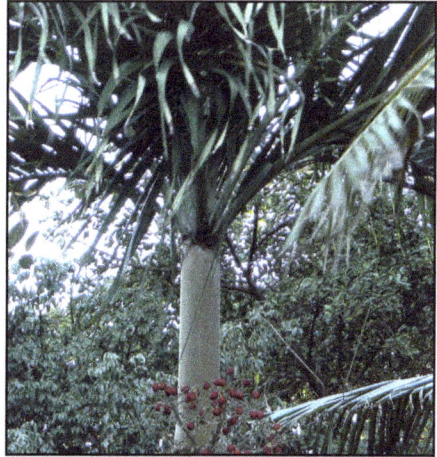

Plant Family: Palmae

Leaves: Pinnate, up to 3 m long, strongly arched; the segments are held in an upright V-shape.

Bark: Smooth, gray, ringed, topped with a 1 m green crownshaft.

Flowers: Yellow, in clusters, appearing in the summer.

Fruits: Rounded, green, turning bright red when mature, to 2 cm, held in clusters just beneath the crownshaft; fall to winter.

Habitat: An attractive non-native that is widely planted; it will sometimes naturalize.

Growth Form: Small to medium-sized tree.

Similar Species: Royal Palm *(Roystonea elata)* also has a green crownshaft, but it has longer leaves, is much larger when mature, and lacks a ringed trunk. Buccaneer Palm *(Psuedophoenix sargentii)* is an endangered species that is rare in its native Keys habitat; it has similar fruits, but has a shorter crownshaft.

Comments: Manila Palm is native to the Philippines; it has long been planted in south Florida as an attractive ornamental.

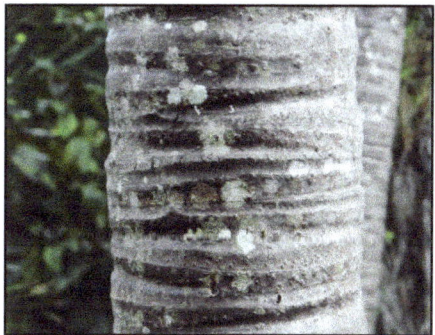

Washingtonia Palm
Washingtonia robusta

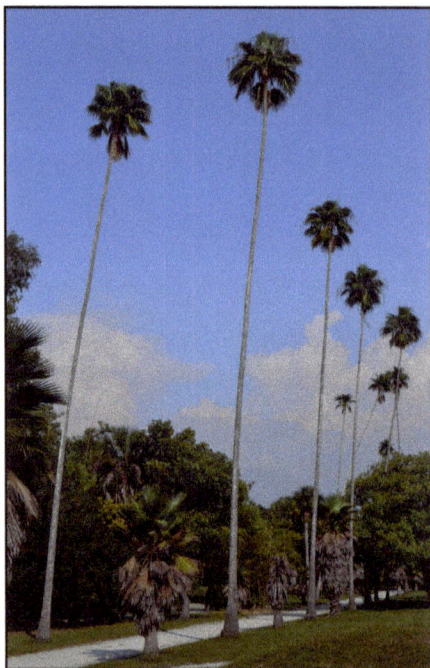

Plant Family: Palmae
Leaves: Palmate, bright green, the leaf segments droop at the tip and the leaf petioles have sharp teeth. The top of the trunk is usually obscured by a dense covering of dead, hanging leaves.
Bark: Gray, blocky and fissured, the solitary trunk bulges a bit at the base.
Flowers: Small, white, in clusters up to 3 m long, seen in the spring.
Fruits: Rounded, brown to black, to 1 cm; summer to fall.
Habitat: Common as an ornamental, this non-native from Mexico may naturalize along roadways and other disturbed sites and is considered moderately invasive.
Growth Form: Medium-sized to large tree.
Similar Species: California Washingtonia *(Washingtonia filifera)* is also planted in south Florida - the trunk is thicker and the leaves are a darker green. The two species hybridize freely so exact identification may be difficult.
Comments: This palm is cold hardy and is also planted in north Florida. The dead leaves may harbor undesirable rodents and some municipalities have passed laws requiring pruning.

Flowering Eudicots – Hardwood Trees

Eudicots are one of the major angiosperm groups, named for the characteristic of the seedlings having two seed leaves. The eudicots include 1) herbaceous annuals that die at the end of each growing season after setting seed, 2) herbaceous perennials, in which the shoot system dies after setting seed but the roots live to regenerate shoots and leaves in the next growing season, and 3) woody perennials, or hardwoods, covered in this book. Woody growth exists above ground all year, the leaves are either deciduous or evergreen, and growth in both height and width is possible, resulting in some truly large specimens.

Shrubs generally have multiple trunks and grow low to the ground, whereas trees have one or two trunks and grow to some height. Although individual authors and the U. S. Forest Service have provided explanations, the reader should know that there is no precise scientific definition of what constitutes a shrub versus a tree. Thus, I have included several woody species that only occasionally reach what most would call tree stature, preferring to err on the side of inclusion.

Within this book the hardwoods are grouped by basic leaf form:

Opposite, compound leaves – These constitute just a few species in south Florida, making identification fairly easy.

Alternate, compound leaves – The largest family in this group are the legumes, related to garden peas and beans. The roots of most legumes have nodules that harbor symbiotic bacteria that fix atmospheric nitrogen in the soil.

Opposite, simple leaves – Probably the most difficult to identify in this group are the Stoppers, which share the characteristics of having flowers with long stamens and fruits that are small berries.

Alternate, simple leaves – This is the largest group; many of the trees, although of different plant families, have similar leaves with pointed drip tips; identification will require more than one feature.

Trees with Opposite, Compound Leaves

Elderberry
Sambucus canadensis

Plant Family: Adoxaceae

Leaves: Opposite, usually once-compound, sometimes twice-compound, with 5 – 7 elliptic, toothed leaflets.

Bark: Brown to gray, with knobby lenticels on younger branches, furrowed on older trunks.

Flowers: White, with 5 petals, individually small, but held in large rounded or flat-topped showy clusters at the branch ends; found in late winter to spring in south Florida, late spring further north in its range.

Fruits: Purple drupes in heavy clusters that are used to make jams and wines; the fruits are seen in summer.

Habitat: Elderberry will be found in wet hammocks and along watercourses where it tends to form thickets.

Growth Form: Shrub to small tree.

Similar Species: Yellow Elder *(Tecoma stans)* is a non-native that sometimes naturalizes; it has similar leaves but has yellow bell-shaped flowers and the fruits are long, thin, legume-like pods.

Comments: Elderberry is an important food plant for birds and other wildlife. It is common in wet habitats throughout the eastern U.S. north into southern Canada.

Caribbean Trumpettree
Tabebuia aurea

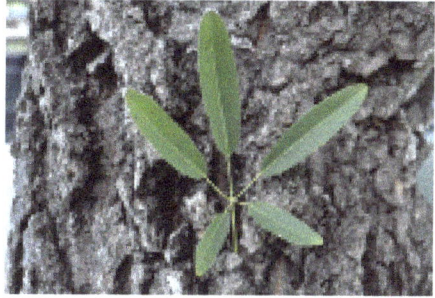

Plant Family: Bignoniaceae

Leaves: Opposite, palmately compound, with 5 (sometimes more) narrow, oblong leaflets that are up to 15 cm long.

Bark: Gray, deeply fissured.

Flowers: Yellow, bell-like, to 10 cm long, in attractive terminal clusters; appearing in early spring, at the end of the dry season.

Fruits: A green pod that ripens to brown, to about 15 cm long; summer.

Habitat: This South American species is planted in yards and gardens for its very showy flower display; it sometimes naturalizes in hammocks and on disturbed ground along the east coast and on the Keys.

Growth Form: Small to medium-sized tree.

Similar Species: White Cedar (*Tabebuia heterophylla*) has purplish white flowers. Schefflera (*Schefflera actinophylla*) has similar, but alternate leaves.

Comments: Caribbean Trumpettree is both salt and drought tolerant.

Carolina Ash
(Pop Ash)
Fraxinus caroliniana

Plant Family: Oleaceae
Leaves: Opposite, once-compound, to 30 cm; 5 to 7 elliptic to obovate leaflets with lightly toothed or wavy margins; the terminal leaflet is often larger and more rounded than the others.
Bark: Medium gray to brown, fissured, usually with lichens present, the base of the trunk may be swollen.
Flowers: Dioecious, small, greenish, appearing in clusters on older parts of the stem from late winter to spring.
Fruits: A samara, typical of ash trees, varying green to purple, that holds a single seed; resembles the blade of a canoe paddle; to 6 cm long; seen spring to summer.
Habitat: Swamps, wet hammocks, and other wetland habitats.
Growth Form: A small to medium-sized tree that sometimes grows in clumps, it is fairly common in hammocks and other wet habitats.
Key Feature: Carolina Ash is the only ash tree found in south Florida, the opposite, compound leaves are diagnostic.
Comments: Carolina Ash is native to the bottomlands and riverbanks of the southeastern U.S.

Torchwood
Amyris elemifera

Plant Family: Rutaceae

Leaves: Opposite, once-compound, 3 (sometimes 5) ovate leaflets with downward curving tips; the stalk of the terminal leaf is longer than those of the other leaflets. Tiny whitish dots are seen on the upper surface.

Bark: Gray to brown, smooth on young specimens, rougher on older trees, often holding lichens. The close-grained, resinous wood has been used for fuel and torches in the Caribbean and in Central America.

Flowers: Small, white, four petals, in attractive terminal clusters; all year, peaking in the early summer.

Fruits: A green drupe that ripens to purple-black, to 1 cm, edible and eaten by birds; fall to winter.

Habitat: Found in and on the edges of eastern coastal hammocks; not at all common.

Growth Form: Shrub to small tree.

Similar Species: Balsam Torchwood (*Amyris balsamifera*) is a similar but rare relative restricted to Keys hammocks.

Comments: Torchwood is important as one of only two food plants of the endangered Schaus' Swallowtail Butterfly.

Lignum Vitae
Guaiacum sanctum

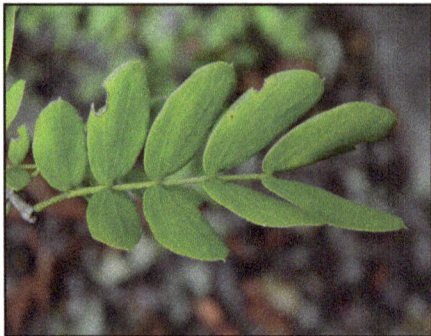

Plant Family: Zygophyllaceae

Leaves: Opposite, once-compound, to 20 cm, with 6 to 10 stalkless oval leaflets, often held in a V-like arrangement, the leaflet apices have a small sharp tip.

Bark: Light gray, rough, blocky on older specimens; the branches on older trees have a distinctly crooked or twisted appearance.

Flowers: Five purple-blue petals with yellow stamens, 1.5 cm in diameter; held in small terminal clusters; mostly spring.

Fruits: A green to orange capsule, to 2 cm; when ripe it opens to reveal dark seeds enclosed in a red pulp; summer to fall.

Habitat: This is a slow growing, but long-lived tree that is restricted to certain drier hammocks on the Keys.

Growth Form: Small tree.

Key Features: Distinguished from other hammock species by the understory form and the opposite, once compound leaves.

Comments: Lignum Vitae is an endangered species that is most common on Lignumvitae Key; it is planted at a few other locations on the Keys and in parks and conservation areas on the peninsula. This beautiful small tree is the national tree of the Bahamas.

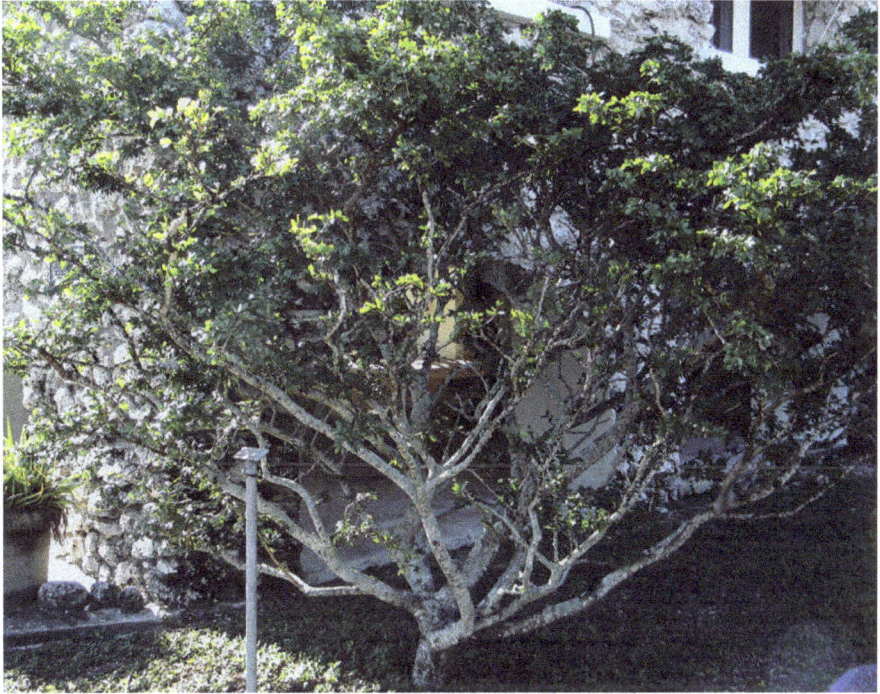

Lignum Vitae Near the Matheson House
on Ligumvitae Key

Trees with alternate, compound leaves

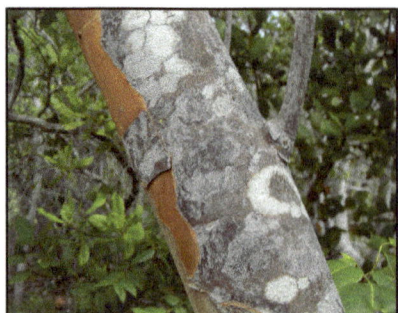

Poisonwood
Metopium toxiferum

Plant Family: Anacardiaceae

Leaves: Alternate, once-compound, with 3 to 7 ovate leaflets, often with black resinous dots.

Bark: Flaky, light gray, with smooth orange under-bark; patches of dark sap may be present on the trunk.

Flowers: Dioecious, small, five petals, creamy white, in loose clusters up to 30 cm long; seen late spring to summer.

Fruits: A yellow-orange drupe, to 1 cm, in loose clusters. Although they are poisonous to humans, certain birds, notably the endangered White-crowned Pigeon, eat the fruits without any apparent harm; late summer to fall.

Habitat: Hammocks and pinelands, it is especially common along the east coast and throughout the Keys.

Growth Form: Small to medium-sized tree.

Key Features: Not likely to be confused with any other south Florida tree, the combination of compound leaves, orange under-bark, and the presence of dark sap on any part of the plant is quite distinctive.

Comments: Poisonwood is a relative of Poison Ivy; leaves, twigs, and bark secrete a dark poisonous sap which can cause skin rashes.

Winged Sumac
Rhus copallinum

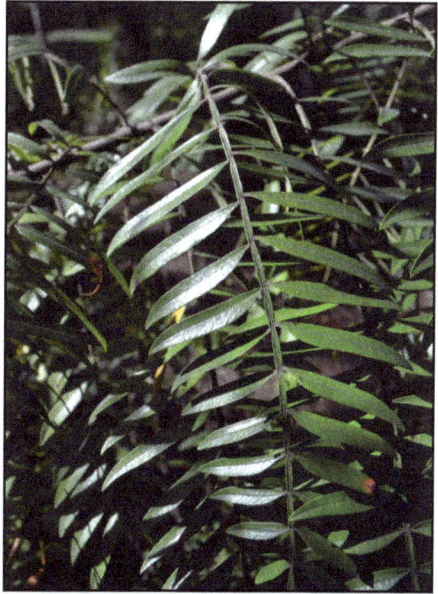

Plant Family: Anacardiaceae

Leaves: Alternate, once-compound, rachis obviously winged, to 30 cm; there are 11 to 25 leaflets which are usually not toothed.

Bark: Brown-gray, rough, with raised lenticels, the U-shaped leaf scars are large and noticeable.

Flowers: Dioecious, yellow-white, in terminal clusters in late summer.

Fruits: Dark red, hairy, individually to 1 cm, but held in large pyramidal terminal clusters; fall to winter.

Habitat: Common in pinelands and a variety of other drier inland habitats, usually not found on the coast.

Growth Form: Deciduous shrub to small tree that tends to form thickets.

Similar Species: Wingleaf Soapberry *(Sapindus saponaria)* has an even number of leaflets numbering 6 to 12; Brazilian Pepper *(Schinus terebinthifolius)* also has fewer leaflets, and smooth fruits.

Comments: Winged Sumac is an important food plant for many birds, which eat the seeds, and for deer and small mammals, which browse the leaves and twigs.

Brazilian Pepper
Schinus terebinthifolius

Plant Family: Anacardiaceae

Leaves: Alternate, once-compound, winged, to 15 cm, with 5 to 9 lightly toothed elliptic leaflets.

Bark: Light brown and smooth on young trees, fissured on older specimens.

Flowers: Dioecious, small, white, in clusters in the leaf axils; all year, peaking summer to fall.

Fruits: Bright red, in attractive clusters in the leaf axils; eaten and spread by birds; all year, peaking late fall to winter.

Habitat: Found in various habitats, including pinelands, hammocks, coastal areas, and along canal borders; highly invasive.

Growth Form: Shrub to small tree.

Similar Species: Two other south Florida trees might be confused with Brazilian Pepper. Winged Sumac *(Rhus copallinum)* has 11 to 21 leaflets that are usually not toothed. Soapberry *(Sapindus saponaria)* usually has an even number of leaflets.

Comments: Brazilian Pepper was first introduced at the end of the nineteenth century by the USDA; this highly invasive species forms dense thickets that crowd out native vegetation. Eradication efforts have met with only limited success. It is no longer legal for arborists to sell this alien species in Florida.

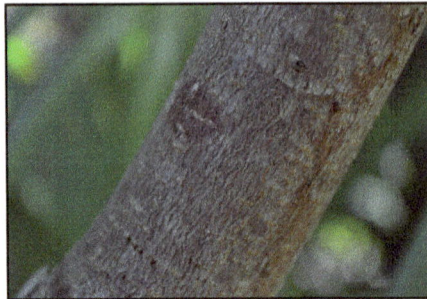

Schefflera
Schefflera actinophylla

Plant Family: Araliaceae

Leaves: Alternate, palmately compound, with 9 to 15 oblong to obovate leaflets, shiny green above, lighter below, the central vein is whitish yellow.

Bark: Gray-brown, smooth on young trees, rougher on older trees. There may be more than one trunk.

Flowers: Red, in long, narrow, attractive racemes extending from the branch ends in summer to early fall.

Fruits: Purple drupes held in long, narrow racemes; late summer to fall.

Habitat: Scheflerra is an Australian species that is used as an indoor ornamental, but is cultivated outdoors in southern Florida, especially on the east coast. It is, however, invasive and may compete with native species.

Growth Form: Small tree to about 10 m tall.

Similar Species: Dwarf Schefflera *(Schefflera arboricola)*, of the same genus, is a Chinese species that is smaller, has fewer leaflets, and yellow flowers. Visitors from the north may know it as a hardy, long-lived, indoor plant.

Comments: Schefflera may grow as an epiphyte on other plants in its native habitat.

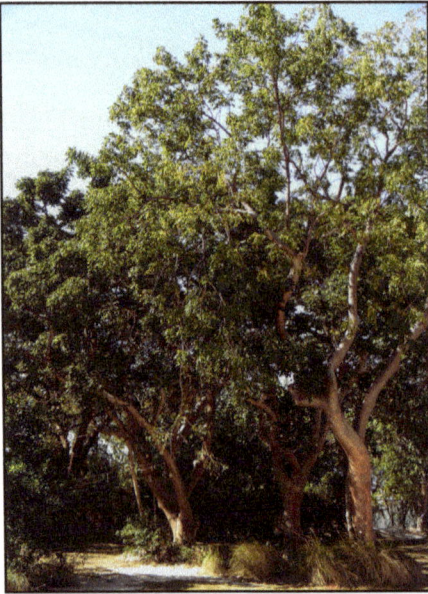

Gumbo Limbo
Bursera simaruba

Plant Family: Burseraceae
Leaves: Alternate, once-compound, with 3 to 9 ovate to elliptic leaflets with sharp pointed apices.
Bark: Copper-colored, with green undertones, flaky; smoother on some specimens.
Flowers: Small, white, in clusters along the branches; spring to summer.
Fruits: Green to reddish brown, three-sided, to 1 cm, with a single white seed inside a red fleshy covering; held in open, short clusters along the branches from fall to winter.
Habitat: Gumbo-Limbo is an important canopy tree in hammocks and is widely planted in south Florida as a very attractive ornamental.
Growth Form: Medium-sized to large tree.
Similar Species: The leaves could possibly be confused with Poisonwood (*Metopium toxiferum*), but the red-brown flaking bark is quite distinctive.
Comments: The bark of Gumbo Limbo is reportedly used as an herbal medicine in the Bahamas, Mexico, and Central and South America to treat skin disorders, and it is steeped to produce a tea to treat various internal maladies. The common name comes from the Spanish "goma elemi," describing the sticky sap.

Sweet Acacia
Acacia farnesiana

Plant Family: Leguminosae

Leaves: Alternate, twice-compound, to 10 cm, with 3 to 6 pairs of segments and 10 - 20 pairs of tiny leaflets per segment.

Bark: Light brown, the zig-zag branches are dark green, with lenticels and long, paired, white spines in the leaf axils; on some specimens the spines are not present.

Flowers: Bright yellow, globular, on long stalks, especially fragrant; typically winter to spring.

Fruits: A thick, shiny, greenish red pod that turns dark brownish purple, to 8 cm long; seen in the summer and fall.

Habitat: Hammocks and pinelands.

Growth Form: A small spreading tree that often has more than one trunk.

Similar Species: Long Spine Acacia *(Acacia macracantha)* is a rare species that also has long thorns but typically has a greater number of segments (10 – 25) comprising each leaf. Twisted Acacia *(Acacia tortuosa)*, also a rare species, has the paired spines fused at the base.

Comments: Sweet Acacia is related to Small's Acacia *(Acacia smallii)*, with some taxonomists considering them a single species. Plant breeders have created several hybrids, usually called Sweet Acacia that are popular ornamentals in the desert southwest for their fragrant flowers and drought tolerance. Sweet Acacia is cultivated in Europe to make perfume.

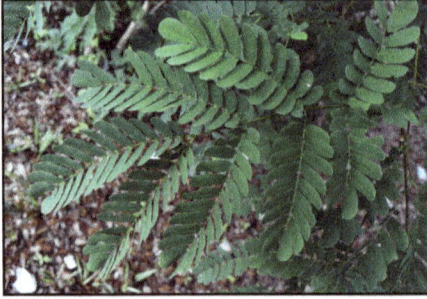

Woman's Tongue
(Lebbeck's Albizia)
Albizia lebbeck

Plant Family: Leguminosae
Leaves: Alternate, twice-compound, with 4 or fewer pairs of opposite segments; the oblong leaflets are fairly large, up to 4 cm long.
Bark: Light brown on young trees, brown with warty protuberances on mature trees.
Flowers: Whitish yellow, with profuse showy stamens; late spring to summer.
Fruits: Flattened, green, ripening to brown, to 25 cm long, with noticeable seedcases; late summer to fall.
Habitat: Planted in yards and gardens, it may escape to disturbed ground and naturalize in south Florida hammocks.
Growth Form: Small to medium-sized tree.
Similar Species: Indian Albizia (*Albizia lebbekoides*) has shorter leaflets, about 2 cm long; Tall Albizia (*Albizia procera*) has 4 or more pairs of opposite segments.
Comments: Woman's Tongue is the most commonly encountered of the three Albizia species; all are from Asia or Australia.

Royal Poinciana
Delonix regia

Plant Family: Leguminosae

Leaves: Alternate, twice-compound, bright green, large, to 50 cm long, with 15 to 25 pairs of segments that hold the tiny leaflets.

Bark: Brown, somewhat rough.

Flowers: Large, red-orange, with five petals, quite showy and noticeable even from a distance, appearing spring to summer.

Fruits: A long green pod that turns dark, to 45 cm; mostly fall to winter, but may persist on the tree for many months.

Habitat: Mostly encountered as an attractive ornamental, it sometimes naturalizes.

Growth Form: Medium-sized tree with a broad spreading crown and a short trunk, commonly planted in yards and along streets.

Key Features: The showy flower clusters and roadside habitat make this tree easy to identify.

Comments: This attractive tree is native to Madagascar where it is considered threatened in the wild. The subspecies *Delonix regia* variety *flavida* has golden-yellow flowers.

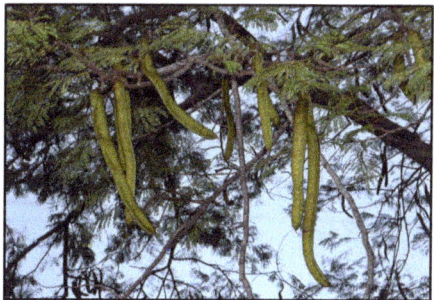

37

Coral Bean
Erythrina herbacea

Plant Family: Leguminosae

Leaves: Alternate, once-compound, light green, with three arrowhead-shaped leaflets. The leaves are shed in winter.

Bark: Gray, smooth, the branches have short prickles.

Flowers: Red, narrow and tubular, to 7 cm, held in showy spikes at the branch ends, attractive to hummingbirds; usually spring to summer, sometimes in the fall.

Fruits: A green pod, turning gray, to 15 cm, with prominent seedcases that hold bright red seeds; appearing in the fall and persisting into winter.

Habitat: Found in hammocks, on sandy soils, and on disturbed sites.

Growth Form: Coral bean is an herbaceous perennial shrub throughout most of its range, which is the coastal plain from the Carolinas west to Texas; in south Florida it is woody and may grow to small tree size.

Key Feature: No other south Florida tree has such distinctive trifoliate leaves.

Comments: The bright red seeds are toxic and are reportedly ground up and used as a rodent poison in Mexico. They are also sometimes fashioned into jewelry but should be kept away from children.

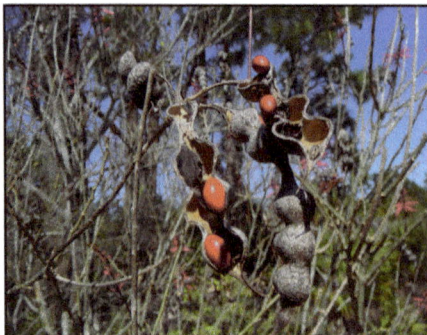

Bahama Lysiloma
(Wild Tamarind)
Lysiloma lattisiliquum

Plant Family: Leguminosae

Leaves: Alternate, twice-compound, to 20 cm, with 2 to 6 pairs of segments and 10 – 20 pairs of leaflets per segment.

Bark: Whitish gray with black; the relatively short trunk is buttressed in large specimens.

Flower: Globular, with numerous white stamens, in the leaf axils; spring to summer.

Fruits: A flattened, short, green pod ripening to black and white, to 10 cm, persisting on the tree for several months.

Habitat: Hammocks, pinelands, commonly planted.

Growth Form: Medium to large tree with a short trunk and a wide spreading crown.

Similar Species: Whitish bark, flat, wide, black and white pods, and no spines on the branches distinguish it from other legumes.

Comments: Large specimens may rival Mahogany in spread.

Jamaica Dogwood
(Fishfuddle Tree)
Piscidia piscipula

Plant Family: Leguminosae

Leaves: Alternate, once-compound, with 5 to 11 oval leaflets, the leaflet margins often turn under; rachis and leaflet stems are yellow. The leaves are gray-green above and whitish gray beneath.

Bark: Light gray, smooth on young trees, becoming rougher on older trees.

Flowers: Pea-like, white to pink, held on stalks in long upright clusters; seen in spring.

Fruits: A green pod that ripens to brown, with four wings, up to 10 cm long, containing reddish brown oval seeds; late summer to fall.

Habitat: Coastal woods and hammocks.

Growth Form: Medium-sized tree.

Key Features: The large oval leaflets and brown, winged fruits distinguish Jamaica Dogwood from other legumes.

Comments: The leaves and bark were formerly used by natives to sedate fish for easier capture. Extracts derived from the tree have been used in herbal medicine to treat a variety of human ailments. Jamaica Dogwood is not related to the true dogwoods; Nelson suggests the common name comes from shipbuilders using the wood for the strong central axis ("dog") of the ship.

Catclaw Blackbead
Pithecellobium unguis-cati

Plant Family: Leguminosae
Leaves: Alternate, compound, with 2 segments and 2 leaflets per segment, each leaflet up to 5 cm long, and having sharp spines at the leaf axils.
Bark: Reddish brown to light brown, rough to lightly fissured.
Flowers: Yellow-white, globular, in showy clusters; late winter to spring.
Fruits: A curved pod that splits open to reveal hard black seeds in a bright red pulp; summer into fall.
Habitat: Sandy soils, hammock edges.
Growth Form: Shrub to small tree.
Key Feature: The unique arrangement of the leaflets allows for easy identification.
Comments: The common name refers to the short spines that are 5 mm long and very sharp, like a cat's claw. Catclaw Blackbead also occurs in Mexico.

Pongam
Millettia pinnata

Plant Family: Leguminosae
Leaves:: Alternate, once-compound, with 5 (sometimes 7) ovate sharp-pointed leaflets; veins whitish.

Bark: Light gray-brown, smooth.

Flowers: Purple-white, pea-like, in narrow spikes from the leaf axils; spring to summer.

Fruits: A flattened elliptic pod to about 5 cm long: green, ripens to brown; fall to winter; may stay on the tree for several months.

Habitat: Native to tropical and warm temperate Asia, planted in yards and parks for its attractive flowers and fruits, it may naturalize on disturbed ground.

Growth Form: Medium-sized to large tree.

Key Features: The large ovate leaflets and elliptic pods will separate Pongam from other legumes.

Comments: Pongam was formerly called *Pongamia pinnata*; the tree is commercially important because the seeds have a high oil content that, although not edible, is used as a lubricant and to produce biodiesel fuel in Asian countries.

Necklace Pod
Sophora tomentosa

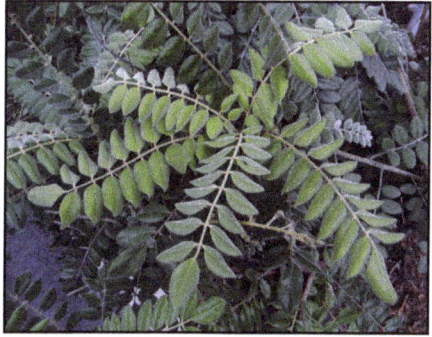

Plant Family: Leguminosae
Leaves: Alternate, once-compound, with 11 to 21 leaflets, the rachis is orange.
Bark: Brown with whitish lenticels, and multiple trunks.
Flowers: Bright yellow, pea-like, quite showy, in terminal spikes; any time of year, peaking in early spring to summer.
Fruits: A greenish yellow pod with prominent, constricted seed cases; fall to winter.
Habitat: Hammock edges, coastal scrub, often planted as an ornamental.
Growth Form: Usually a multi-stemmed shrub, it may sometimes attain small tree stature.
Similar Species: Necklace Pod has two subspecies – *Sophora tomentosa* variety *truncata* is a Florida native with shiny, hairless leaves – *Sophora tomentosa* variety *occidentalis* (as shown) is native to Texas and has densely hairy leaves. The non-native subspecies is more commonly planted.
Comments: This attractive plant is often planted as an ornamental shrub. Look for it in state parks and private plantings, especially on the Keys. The flowers attract bees, butterflies, and hummingbirds; the seeds, however, are known to be mildly toxic if ingested.

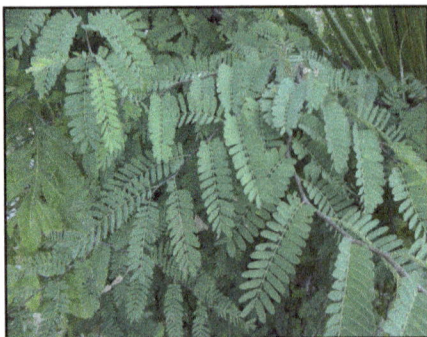

Tamarind
Tamarindus indica

Plant Family: Leguminosae
Leaves: Alternate, once-compound, with 10 – 16 pairs of oblong leaflets; the leaves are held on zigzag branches.
Bark: Medium to dark gray, lightly fissured.
Flowers: Yellow, pea-like, the petals show red streaks; late summer to fall.
Fruits: A green pod that turns brown, to 10 cm long, the pulp that surrounds the seeds is edible; fall to winter.
Habitat: Typically found along the coast as an escape from cultivation. It is long-lived and its presence often indicates the site of former homesteads, where it was planted for shade and its fruits.
Growth Form: Medium-sized to large tree.
Similar Species: The lightly fissured trunk and characteristic zigzag branches distinguish it from other legumes.
Comments: This non-native species originated in Africa but has been introduced to tropical countries worldwide, especially India, which explains the specific name. Tamarind has many culinary and medicinal uses and is considered one of the most useful plants to human societies.

Mahogany
Swietenia mahagoni

Plant Family: Meliaceae

Leaves: Alternate, once-compound, with 4 to 10 sickle-shaped leaflets; rachis and petioles bright yellow; the leaflets are asymmetric, the lower part is smaller than the upper part.

Bark: Reddish brown, rough and blocky.

Flowers: Small, five petals, greenish white with a yellow center; seen in the spring into summer.

Fruits: A large, brown, five-part, egg-shaped capsule, to 12 cm; when ripe it splits at the base to release the light airborne seeds; mostly fall into winter.

Habitat: The natural habitat of Mahogany is tropical hammocks, but it is also commonly planted in south Florida along streets and highways.

Growth Form: Mahogany is a long-lived and potentially large tree with an impressive spread; in the open it may be as wide as it is tall.

Key Features: The large size, the sickle-shaped leaflets, and the large fruits make this magnificent tree easy to identify.

Comments: Formerly heavily harvested for its prized wood, it is now protected by law and listed as threatened in the wild.

Bischofia
(Bishopwood)
Bischofia javanica

Plant Family: Phyllanthus
Leaves: Alternate, once-compound, with three finely toothed elliptic leaflets that have pointed apices; the veins follow the leaf margins; sap is milky.
Bark: Light brown on young trees, darker brown on mature trees, rough and scaly.
Flowers: Dioecious, whitish yellow, individually small, but held in large hanging clusters from the branches; spring to summer.
Fruits: Green capsules that ripen to dark orange or dark blue, to 1 cm in diameter, in large hanging clusters from the branches, eaten by birds which spread the seeds; summer to fall.
Habitat: Invasive in a variety of habitats - hammocks, low woods, disturbed ground, often in damp situations.
Growth Form: Medium-sized to large tree.
Key Feature: The compound leaves with long petioles that always have three leaflets are distinctive.
Comments: Native to India, Southeast Asia and Indonesia, where it is an important commercial species that is used for charcoal production, to make paper pulp, in construction, and to make a red dye.

Bitterbush
Picramnia pentandra

Plant Family: Picramniaceae
Leaves: Alternate, once-compound, to 30 cm, with 5 to 9 ovate leaflets that have long pointed apices.
Bark: Brown, smooth on young specimens, rougher on older trees.
Flowers: Dioecious, very small, green, in long drooping clusters; appearing spring to fall, peaking in midsummer.
Fruits: A red to purple-black berry, about 1 cm long, held on red stalks in dense clusters; summer to fall.
Habitat: Hammock edges and understory, sandy soils.
Growth Form: Shrub to small tree.
Similar Species: The bark, flowers and fruits are similar to Paradise Tree *(Simarouba glauca)*, but Bitterbush differs in that the leaflets have pointed apices and are 9 or fewer per leaf, and the growth form is generally shrubby.
Comments: The inner bark, leaves, and fruits of this endangered species have a bitter taste. In the Bahamas and West Indies a tonic is produced from extracts of the tree to treat gastrointestinal problems.

Southern Prickly Ash
(Hercules' Club)
Zanthoxylum clava-herculis

Plant Family: Rutaceae

Leaves: Alternate, once-compound, with an odd number of leaflets, 7 or more; the paired leaflets are asymmetric and the margins have rounded teeth; paired prickles are found along the rachis.

Bark: Light gray with prominent warty and prickly knobs.

Flowers: Dioecious, small, green-yellow, in clusters at the branch ends; seen in spring.

Fruits: Green to brown follicles at the branch ends, each holding a shiny, black seed; summer into fall.

Habitat: Coastal hammocks, sandy soils.

Growth Form: Small tree.

Similar Species: Wild Lime Prickly Ash *(Zanthoxylum fagara)* has winged leaves with rounded leaflets.

Comments: Southern Prickly Ash ranges west to Texas and north along the coast to the mid-Atlantic states.

Biscayne Prickly Ash
Zanthoxylum coriaceum

Plant Family: Rutaceae

Leaves: Alternate, once-compound, to 20 cm, with an even number of thick leaflets (2 to 8) that have rounded apices.

Bark: Dark gray, rough, small prickles are present on the branches.

Flowers: Dioecious, small, yellow, in dense clusters at the branch ends; seen in spring.

Fruits: Green to brown follicles at the branch ends, each holding a shiny, black seed; summer to fall.

Habitat: Sandy and limestone soils of the east coast; several trees have been re-introduced to Miami Beach parks in recent years.

Growth Form: Shrub to small tree.

Similar Species: The other species of *Zanthozylum* (Prickly Ash, Wild Lime Prickly Ash) have an odd number of leaflets.

Comments: Biscayne Prickly Ash is a rare tree that is considered an endangered species; however, it will be found planted in yards and botanical gardens. It is a host plant to the endangered Schaus' Swallowtail butterfly.

Wild Lime Prickly Ash
Zanthoxylum fagara

Plant Family: Rutaceae

Leaves: Alternate, once-compound, the petiole and rachis are obviously winged, with 7 to 11 rounded leaflets.

Bark: Light brown, sharp prickles are present on the branches and trunk.

Flowers: Dioecious, small, greenish-yellow, in short, dense clusters in the leaf axils; spring.

Fruits: Green to brown follicles in the leaf axils, each contains a single black seed; summer to fall.

Habitat: Found in the understory and on the edges of south Florida and Keys hammocks.

Growth Form: Shrub to small tree.

Similar Species: Distinguished from other *Zanthoxylum* species by the winged leaves with an odd number of leaflets.

Comments: Wild Lime is a shrubby tree that ranges north in Florida to the central part of the state; it also occurs in Texas and Mexico; the crushed leaves have an aroma of limes; it is a host plant for the Giant Swallowtail butterfly.

Yellow Heart
(Satinwood)
Zanthoxylum flavum

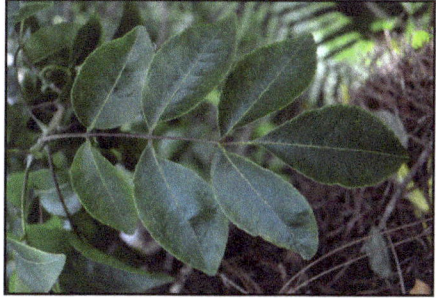

Plant Family: Rutaceae

Leaves: Alternate, once-compound, with 5 – 9 ovate to elliptic leaflets.

Bark: Light gray, smooth.

Flowers: Dioecious, small, yellow, in dense clusters at the branch ends; appearing in the summer.

Fruits: Green to brown follicles at the branch ends, each holding a shiny, black seed; present in the fall.

Habitat: Keys hammocks.

Growth Form: Medium-sized tree.

Similar Species: Yellow Heart is the only *Zanthozylum* species that lacks prickles on the trunk and branches.

Comments: Yellow Heart is native to the West Indies and the Bahamas, it is quite rare on the Keys, however it will be found planted in south Florida botanical gardens. The common names come from the golden brown, slightly oily, and dense wood which is prized for its beauty and commercial value.

Inkwood
Exothea paniculata

Plant Family: Sapindaceae

Leaves: Alternate, once-compound, with 4 (sometimes 6) shiny, elliptic leaflets.

Bark: Light gray-brown, roughened.

Flowers: Dioecious, small, with five petals, white with an orange center, held in clusters; from late winter to early spring.

Fruits: A red to purple-black berry, 1 cm in diameter; from late spring to early summer.

Habitat: Fairly common in coastal hammocks and on limestone soils.

Growth Form: Small to medium-sized tree.

Similar Species: Alternate, compound leaves, with only 4 leaflets is a characteristic only shared with Catclaw Blackbead *(Pithecellobium unguis catti)*; however, the leaflet shape and arrangement differs.

Comments: The crushed fruits are used in the West Indies to produce a dark ink.

Tulipwood
Harpullia arborea

Plant Family: Sapindaceae

Leaves: Alternate, once-compound, with an even (sometimes odd) number of elliptic leaflets that are held alternately on the rachis.

Bark: Light brown, smooth to somewhat flaky, the trunk is fluted at the base.

Flowers: Monoecious, whitish yellow, in loose clusters from the leaf axils; spring to summer.

Fruits: A yellow two-lobed capsule about 4 cm long that ripens to bright red and splits to reveal 2 dark seeds; from late summer into fall.

Habitat: Hammocks and disturbed sites in Miami-Dade County.

Growth Form: Large tree.

Key Features: The combination of once-compound leaves and unique red-orange fruits will identify Tulipwood.

Comments: Tulipwood is native to India, Southeast Asia, and the Philippines; indigenous people have used the bark as a fish poison.

White Ironwood
Hypelate trifoliata

Plant Family: Sapindaceae
Leaves: Alternate, once-compound, with 3 glossy, obovate leaflets in a clover-like arrangement, the apices are sometimes notched.
Bark: Gray or brown, smooth on young trees, somewhat rougher on older trees.
Flowers: Monoecious, small, white, held on stalks in open axillary and terminal clusters; spring to summer.
Fruits: A green drupe that ripens to black, to 1 cm diameter; summer into fall.
Habitat: Hammocks and pinelands.
Growth Form: Small tree.
Key Feature: The alternate, compound leaves, with only 3 leaflets are the unique feature.
Comments: White Ironwood is an endangered species in Florida that was formerly over-harvested for its close-grained, valuable wood; it is more common on the islands of the Caribbean.

Soapberry
(Wingleaf Soapberry)
Sapindus saponaria

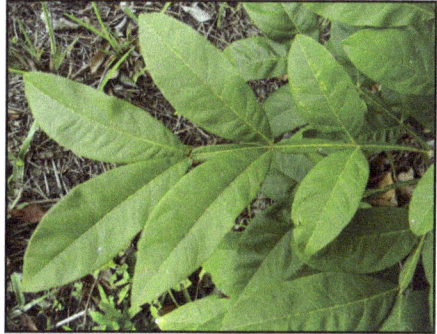

Plant Family: Sapindaceae

Leaves: Alternate, once-compound, winged, with 6 to 8 elliptic leaflets; sometimes there is a terminal leaflet.

Bark: Gray to tan-colored, smooth on young trees, becoming rougher with reddish brown patches on older trees.

Flowers: Monoecious, small, cream colored, in loose terminal panicles; summer into fall.

Fruits: Orange-brown berries called soap nuts, to 2 cm in diameter, enclosing a single black seed; fall to winter and persisting for several weeks.

Habitat: Hammocks, coastal scrub.

Growth Form: Small tree.

Key Feature: The alternate, compound leaves with a winged rachis separate it from other hammock trees.

Comments: Soapberry ranges south to the West Indies, Mexico, and Central and South America. The generic name *Sapindus* means "soap of the Indians"; the berries contain saponin, a natural soap that can be used on the skin or as a laundry detergent. Native people have also used it medicinally to treat skin disorders.

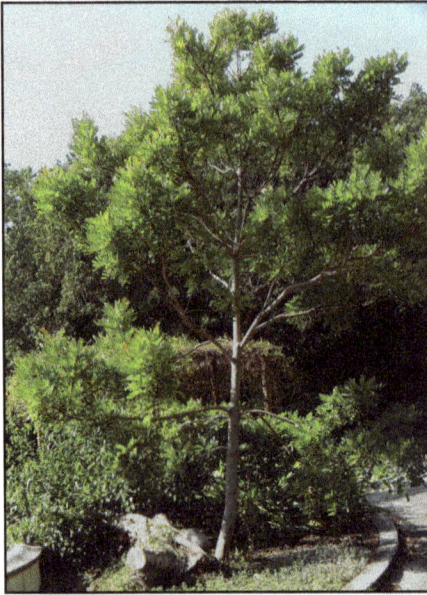

Paradise Tree
Simarouba glauca

Plant Family: Simaroubaceae

Leaves: Alternate, once-compound, with 10 to 14 oval to oblong leaflets, glossy green above, gray beneath; sometimes there is a terminal leaflet (as shown), new growth is shiny red.

Bark: Gray-brown, smooth on younger trees, somewhat rougher on mature trees.

Flowers: Dioecious, yellow, small, in open clusters from the leaf axils; from late winter into spring.

Fruits: A rounded red drupe that ripens to purple-black, to 2.5 cm long, edible and eaten by birds; from late spring into summer.

Habitat: Coastal hammocks, it is also cultivated for its attractive form.

Growth Form: Medium-sized tree.

Key Features: The straight-trunked form (never shrubby) combined with the alternate, shiny, compound leaves with oval leaflets will separate Paradise Tree from other compound leaved species.

Comments: Paradise Tree is a fast-growing tree with a narrow diameter trunk that may reach canopy height. In Central and South America the bark is used as an herbal medicine and the black seeds are harvested to produce vegetable oil for culinary purposes.

Mangroves

South Florida is home to three species of mangroves, tropical trees that are grouped together not because they are closely related, but because of their shared affinity for coastal saltwater environments, and their adaptations to deal with anaerobic soils and excess salt, conditions which most plants cannot tolerate.

Red Mangrove is typically found at the seaward edge of the mangrove zone and is characterized by reddish-brown prop roots. This species has the ability to exclude much of the salt in the water from entering the roots.

Black Mangrove is commonly found shoreward of Red Mangrove, but the two may also share habitat. An extensive network of breathing roots called pneumatophores project from the mud around each tree, helping to aerate the roots.

White Mangrove is usually found the furthest inland; it may also have breathing roots, as well as lenticels on the lower trunk to facilitate gas exchange. Both white and black mangrove are salt excreters, glands on the leaves excrete a highly saline solution; when the water evaporates salt crystals form on the leaf surface.

Mangrove forests provide many ecological services - mangroves act to trap sediments and stabilize shorelines; they are nursery grounds for fish and aquatic invertebrates, several of which are important to both commercial and sport fisheries; birds nest among the branches and feed on adjacent mudflats, in fact, mangrove ecosystems are among the most biologically productive on earth, rivaled only by coral reefs and tropical rainforests.

Trees with Opposite, Simple Leaves

Black Mangrove
Avicennia germinans

Plant Family: Acanthaceae

Leaves: Opposite, simple, elliptic, to about 10 cm, green above, grayish below, salt crystals are commonly present on the surface (as shown).

Bark: Black with small blocks; upright breathing roots called pneumatophores are present in the mud surrounding each tree.

Flowers: White, with four petals, in terminal clusters, quite fragrant, from which bees make a prized honey; throughout the year, peaking in the summer months.

Fruits: A flattened, green, pointed pod, to 4 cm long; all year, peaking in the fall.

Habitat: Coastal zone, mudflats, it may share habitat with Red Mangrove *(Rhizophora mangle)* but it is also found inland of that species.

Growth Form: A shrub to small tree in Florida, it grows larger further south in the tropics.

Key Features: Of the mangroves, it has leaves green above, whitish gray beneath, black bark, and many breathing roots.

Comments: Black Mangrove has a widespread distribution, occurring on the coasts of Florida, the Bahamas, the West Indies, Central and South America, the Galapagos Islands, and West Africa.

White Mangrove
Laguncularia racemosa

Plant Family: Combretaceae

Leaves: Opposite, simple, oval to oblong, fairly thick, apices rounded, pointed, or slightly notched, to 10 cm, light green above and below; look for two very small salt-excreting glands at the base of the leaf.

Bark: Brown to gray, fissured; breathing roots may be present, but not to the extent found in Black Mangrove.

Flowers: Dioecious, white, very small, fragrant, bell-shaped, with 5 petals, in spikes at the twig ends; typically spring into summer.

Fruits: Green to light gray-brown, broader at the apex, 2 cm long, with longitudinal ribs; holding a single seed; summer into fall.

Habitat: Coastal, at the landward edge of the mangrove zone.

Growth Form: A shrub to small tree in Florida, it grows larger further south in the tropics.

Key Features: Of the mangroves, White Mangrove has leaves the same light green color both above and below.

Comments: The root system of White Mangrove is shallow but dense, trapping sediment and preventing erosion, however, lacking prop roots, it is less resistant to hurricanes than Red Mangrove.

Australian Pine
(Beefwood)
Casuarina equisetifolia

Plant Family: Casuarinaceae
Leaves: Vestigial, very tiny and whorled, requiring a lens for observation, and held at regular nodes on twigs that resemble pine needles. The twigs are the photosynthetic structures of the tree.
Bark: Gray, with patches of coppery under-bark, rough, often peeling in long strips. The roots fix nitrogen in the soil.
Flowers: Very small, at the twig ends and along the twigs; any time of year.
Fruits: Small nuts, which aggregate on rounded brown cones.
Habitat: Coastal, and along canals; highly salt tolerant.
Growth Form: Medium-sized to large tree with a straight trunk, often in single species stands.
Similar Species: Australian Pine is non-native, and is the most common of the three *Casuarina* species in south Florida; all are very similar to one another, and all are invasive.
Comments: This weedy species with a dense root system was first brought to Florida for use as windbreaks along canal banks and developed shorelines; it is now common in coastal sandy soils and a variety of other habitats, where it crowds out and shades out native species.

Autograph Tree
(Pitch Apple)
Clusia rosea

Plant Family: Clusiaceae

Leaves: Opposite, simple, obovate, thick and leathery, to 18 cm, dark green above, lighter below, apices broadly rounded.

Bark: Light brown with lenticels, large leaf scars are present on the branches.

Flowers: The showy flowers have white and pink petals and a yellow center; mostly summer, sometimes at other times of the year.

Fruits: Round, fairly large, to 8 cm in diameter, green ripening to brown, they split to reveal red, pulpy seeds that attract birds; seen in fall.

Habitat: Native to hammocks of the West Indies, uncommonly found in Keys hammocks, leading some botanists to question its status as a Florida native; widely planted on the Keys.

Growth Form: A small to medium-sized shrubby tree that may start as an epiphyte on another tree.

Similar Species: Seven-year Apple *(Genipa clusifolia)* has brighter green shiny leaves.

Comments: Marks made on the surface of the thick leaves will remain for some time. Autograph tree is drought resistant and salt tolerant.

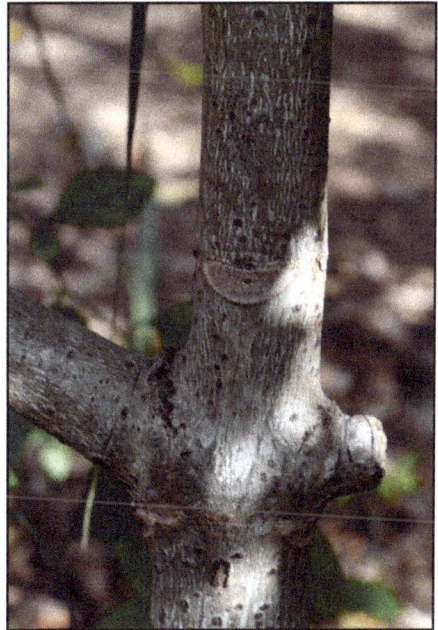

Beautyberry
Callicarpa americana

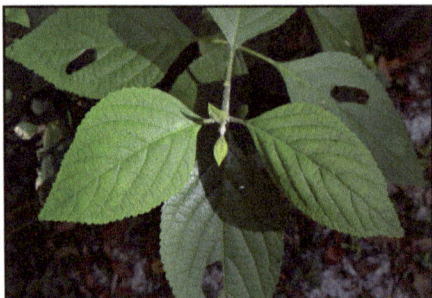

Plant Family: Lamiaceae

Leaves: Opposite, simple, ovate, margins lightly toothed, to 15 cm; the veins are noticeable and follow the leaf edges.

Bark: Light brown, smooth, with raised lenticels; has multiple trunks when growing in the understory of hammocks, has one or just a few trunks when growing in full sun.

Flowers: Small, pink, in tight clusters in the leaf axils; appearing spring into summer.

Fruits: Bright purple-red drupes in attractive clusters in the leaf axils; eaten by birds and other animals, thus distributing the seeds; appearing late summer and persisting on the branches for several weeks. A cultivated variety has white fruits.

Habitat: Beautyberry is a generalist species that is at home in a number of different habitats, including hammocks, pinelands, open woods, and disturbed sites; it is also commonly cultivated.

Growth Form: Shrub to small tree.

Key Feature: The dense clusters of purple-red fruits easily identify this common species.

Comments: Beautyberry ranges north to Maryland and west to Arkansas. Cold hardy cultivars will be found planted as far north as Massachusetts. It was formerly placed in the Verbenaceae family.

Locust Berry
Byrsonima lucida

Plant Family: Malpighiaceae

Leaves: Opposite, simple, stiff, oblanceolate, to 6 cm, dark green above, whitish green below, the petioles are swollen where they grasp the stem.

Bark: Mottled gray, smooth, the twigs are light brown.

Flowers: White to pink, stalked, with 5 petals, turning red as they mature; in attractive standing clusters (flower buds are shown); spring to early summer.

Fruits: Green drupes, ripening to red-brown, to 1 cm, edible; seen in summer.

Habitat: Pinelands, hammock edges.

Growth Form: Shrub to small tree.

Key Features: The small, opposite, oblanceolate leaves that are light green beneath and that clasp the light brown stems are diagnostic.

Comments: Locust Berry is an uncommon understory shrub in South Florida pinelands; it may attain small tree size on the Keys. It is listed as a threatened species in Florida.

Florida Tetrazygia
Tetrazygia bicolor

Plant Family: Melastomataceae

Leaves: Opposite, simple, glossy, lanceolate, to 15 cm, with 3 prominent and depressed lengthwise veins.

Bark: Light brown, rough to lightly fissured.

Flowers: White, with five petals and yellow stamens in attractive terminal clusters that appear in the spring and into summer.

Fruits: A purple-black berry, to 1 cm, clustered at the branch ends, edible; late summer to fall.

Habitat: Pinelands, hammock edges.

Growth Form: Shrub to small tree.

Key Feature: The three prominent, lengthwise leaf veins are unique, making this species easy to identify in any habitat.

Comments: Florida Tetrazygia is mostly found in the pinelands of South Florida as a shrub, but it may reach small tree status within hammocks; it is found in full sun on hammock edges in a shrubby form in single species thickets.

64

Myrtle-of-the-River
Calyptranthes zuzygium

Plant Family: Myrtaceae
Leaves: : Opposite, simple, ovate to elliptic, to 6 cm, apices blunt pointed, the midrib is noticeably raised above the leaf surface, especially towards the base; the crushed leaves have a pleasant aroma. The tip of each twig terminates in a pair of leaves, an arrangement unique to the genus.
Bark: Gray, smooth on young trees, fissured on older trees.
Flowers: Green to white, in clusters at the twig ends; the stamens are numerous and the flowers lack petals; the flower buds are initially capped by a lid-like cover which is shed on flowering; appearing in spring into summer.
Fruits: A yellow berry that ripens to red or purple-black, to 1 cm in diameter; summer to fall.
Habitat: Hammock understory.
Growth Form: Shrub to small tree.
Similar Species: In the closely related Pale Lidflower (*Calyptranthes pallens*) the midrib is not raised above the leaf surface.
Comments: Myrtle of the River is listed as an endangered species in Florida.

White Stopper
Eugenia axillaris

Plant Family: Myrtaceae

Leaves: Opposite, simple, ovate, paler beneath, somewhat blunt pointed, to 6 cm, the leaf edges turn up, the crushed leaves may have a distinctive musky odor.

Bark: Light gray, blocky.

Flowers: White, small, in short clusters in the leaf axils; like the other Eugenia species they appear fuzzy due to the many stamens and they attract butterflies and other pollinators; mostly seen in summer, also at other times of the year.

Fruits: A red berry that ripens to black, to 1 cm, in the leaf axils, edible; may stay on the tree for many weeks; summer to fall.

Habitat: Hammock understory.

Growth Form: Shrub to small tree.

Similar Species: This is probably the most common *Eugenia* species in south Florida hammocks. The skunk-like odor of the crushed leaves distinguishes it from others of that genus.

Comments: The conspicuous fruits are relished by birds and small mammals. If the leaves of members of the Myrtaceae are held to the light many tiny glands will be seen. These hold the aromatic oils that produce fragrance when the leaves are crushed.

Red-Berry Stopper
Eugenia confusa

Plant Family: Myrtaceae

Leaves: Opposite, simple, glossy, ovate to elliptic, to 8 cm, the apices are very long-pointed. Like all of the stoppers the new leaves are red, turning light green, and finally darker green.

Bark: Light gray with brown, fissured.

Flowers: White, small, with numerous stamens, held in short clusters in the leaf axils; mostly summer, also at other times of the year.

Fruits: A red to purple berry, to 1 cm, held in the leaf axils, edible.

Fruit Date: Summer to fall.

Habitat: Hammock understory of south Florida and the Keys; it is considered an endangered species.

Growth Form: Small to medium-sized tree.

Key Feature: The very long-pointed apices of the leaves, more so than any of the Stoppers, are the key feature.

Comments: This attractive species is the tallest of the Stoppers, sometimes reaching canopy height.

Spanish Stopper
(Boxleaf Stopper)
Eugenia foetida

Plant Family: Myrtaceae

Leaves: Opposite, simple, elliptic to obovate, paler beneath, to 6 cm, apices more rounded than other *Eugenia* species; the crushed leaves are aromatic.

Bark: Light brown to gray, smooth to lightly fissured.

Flowers: White, small, in short clusters in the leaf axils, the stamens are long and profuse; summer, also at other times of the year.

Fruits: A red to black berry, to 1 cm, held in the leaf axils, edible; summer to fall.

Habitat: Hammock understory, also sometimes found in the pinelands of the Keys.

Growth Form: Small tree.

Similar Species: Spanish Stopper is distinguished from other *Eugenia* species by having the most rounded leaf apices.

Comments: Spanish Stopper is a fairly common hammock understory tree, close to White Stopper *(Eugenia axillaris)* in abundance.

Red Stopper
Eugenia rhombea

Plant Family: Myrtaceae

Leaves: Opposite, simple, ovate, paler beneath, long pointed, to 6 cm, the leaf petioles and leaf margins are yellow. The crushed leaves have an odor of menthol.

Bark: Light mottled gray, smooth, usually with multiple trunks.

Flowers: White, small, with profuse stamens, found in short clusters in the leaf axils; mostly summer, also at other times of the year.

Fruits: A red to black berry to 1 cm, held in the leaf axils, edible; summer to fall.

Habitat: Rockland hammock understory, quite rare in the wild; it is a slow growing species that nevertheless does well in cultivation.

Growth Form: Small tree.

Similar Species: The leaf apices are long pointed, but to a lesser degree than Red-berry Stopper *(Eugenia confusa)*.

Comments: Red Stopper is an endangered species, most common in nature at stations on Key Largo and on Elliot Key; it is planted at other sites on the Keys and grows well in private plantings.

Surinam Cherry
Eugenia uniflora

Plant Family: Myrtaceae

Leaves: Opposite, simple, ovate, with very short petioles, green and glossy above, paler beneath, to 8 cm; new leaves have an attractive copper or burgundy color.

Bark: Brown, rough, with smooth light brown under-bark.

Flowers: White, small, with profuse stamens, found in short clusters in the leaf axils; some flowers are found singly; present throughout the year.

Fruits: A green ridged berry, to 3 cm, that ripens to dark red, edible; seen at any time of the year.

Habitat: Naturalized in coastal hammocks, also commonly planted as a hedge or screen.

Growth Form: Shrub to small tree.

Key Feature: The leaves with very short petioles and the red, ridged fruits will distinguish Surinam Cherry from other species in the family Myrtaceae.

Comments: Surinam Cherry is a non-native species from coastal Brazil where it is known as Pitanga. It has been introduced to many tropical countries for its attractive foliage and edible fruits, but it is invasive and tends to crowd out native species.

Long-Stalked Stopper
Mosiera longipes

Plant Family: Myrtaceae
Leaves: Opposite, simple, shiny, ovate, small, to only about 3 cm, apices blunt pointed.
Bark: Light gray, smooth, with multiple trunks.
Flowers: White, with 4 petals, on very long stalks, with numerous stamens; mostly spring into summer.
Fruits: Green, ripening to black, to 1 cm, on very long stalks; summer to fall.
Habitat: Mostly found in pinelands, especially on the Keys, sometimes found on the edges or in the understory of hammocks.
Growth Form: Typically a shrub in the pinelands, a small tree in hammocks.
Similar Species: The very long stalks of the flowers and fruits combined with the small leaves separate it from other Stoppers.
Comments: Long-Stalked Stopper is listed as a threatened species in Florida. Older references place Long-Stalked Stopper in the genus *Eugenia*.

Twinberry Stopper
(Simpson's Stopper)
Myrcianthes fragrans

Plant Family: Myrtaceae
Leaves: Opposite, simple, elliptic, leathery, blunt-pointed, to 8 cm; the crushed leaves are pleasantly aromatic, some say with an odor of nutmeg.
Bark: Light brown to red-brown, smooth to somewhat flaky.
Flowers: White, small, on long stalks in the leaf axils, the stamens are long and numerous. Like all the Stoppers, the flowers attract insect pollinators; all year, peaking in summer.
Fruits: An orange-red berry to 1 cm, usually two per leaf axil, edible; summer to fall.
Habitat: Hammock understory, uncommon on the Keys.
Growth Form: Small to medium-sized tree.
Similar Species: The light brown to red-brown, lightly peeling bark, combined with the elliptic, blunt-pointed leaves should distinguish it from other Stoppers.
Comments: Twinberry Stopper was formerly classified as *Eugenia simpsonii*. Nelson reports that this species is quite cold tolerant, surviving night temperatures below freezing.

Blolly
Guapira discolor

Plant Family: Nyctaginaceae

Leaves: Opposite, simple, elliptic to obovate, glossy, to 8 cm, light green, edges wavy, apices rounded, central vein yellow and translucent when backlit (as shown); the leaf petioles are yellow and distinctly grooved.

Bark: Light gray, fairly smooth, yellow lichens are often present.

Flowers: Dioecious, very small, greenish white, lacking petals, in small clusters at the twig ends; from late spring into summer.

Fruits: Scarlet red, to 1.5 cm, found at the twig ends, edible; summer into fall.

Habitat: Fairly common in coastal hammocks and thickets, less commonly found in pinelands.

Growth Form: Shrub to small tree, it tends to form thickets.

Key Features: Distinguished from other opposite leaved hammock species by having grooved leaf petioles and translucent leaf midribs.

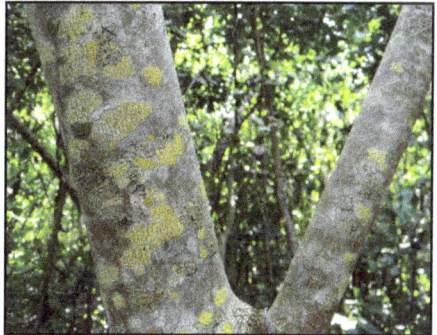

Comments: The fruits are favored by the endangered White-crowned Pigeon. The name Blolly is short for loblolly, which is an Old English term for a bog or a swamp, and the thicket forming trees that grow there.

Pisonia
(Cockspur)
Pisonia rotundata

Plant Family: Nyctaginaceae
Leaves: Opposite, simple, to 10 cm, oval, the apices may be notched or rounded, the veins are yellow and noticeable.
Bark: Light mottled gray, fairly smooth.
Flowers: Dioecious, very small, greenish white, lacking petals, in short, dense clusters at the twig ends; present in the spring
Fruits: Small, light brown, very sticky; from summer into fall.
Habitat: Restricted to Keys hammocks and thickets; Pisonia is an endangered species that is probably most common on Big Pine Key.
Growth Form: Shrub to small tree.
Key Features: The oval leaves with obvious straight, yellow veins should distinguish Pisonia from other opposite leaved Keys trees.
Comments: The genus is named after Dutch naturalist Willem Piso. The small, sticky seeds are an adaptation that allows them to adhere to the feathers of birds, thus dispersing the seeds to new habitats.

Black Ironwood
(Leadwood)
Krugiodendron ferreum

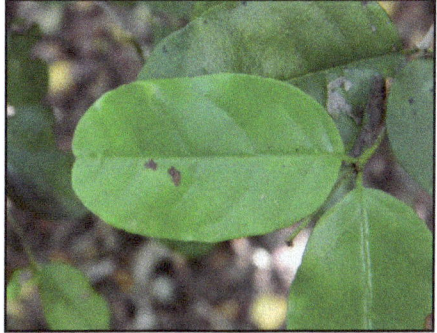

Plant Family: Rhamnaceae
Leaves: Opposite, simple, oval to ovate, flexible, glossy green above, lighter green below, apices often notched, to 4 cm; the margins are somewhat wavy; the short petioles have fine hairs. New growth has a golden-green color.
Bark: Medium gray, scaly and fissured.
Flowers: Small, yellow, in sparse clusters in the leaf axils; typically spring, but may appear at other times of the year.
Fruits: An oval drupe to 1 cm, green, ripening to purple-black, held in the leaf axils, edible; usually summer to fall.
Habitat: Coastal hammocks.
Growth Form: Shrub to small tree.
Similar Species: The related Darling Plum *(Reynosia septentrionalis)* has similar leaves, but they are stiff, not flexible like Black Ironwood.
Comments: The wood of this species is hard and durable; it has a greater density than any other North American tree and readily sinks in water! Black Ironwood is also found in the West Indies and along the east coast of Mexico and Central America.

Darling Plum
(Red Ironwood)
Reynosia septentrionalis

Plant Family: Rhamnaceae
Leaves: Opposite, simple, oblong to elliptic, to 4 cm, stiff and leathery, the leaf apices are blunt or more commonly notched.
Bark: Gray to brown, becoming fissured with age.
Flowers: Very small, greenish yellow, with 5 sepals but no petals, held on stalks that originate from the leaf axils; all year, peaking in spring and summer.
Fruits: A purple-black drupe, to 2 cm, edible and tasting like blueberries; mostly summer to fall, but may appear at other times of the year.
Habitat: Limited to hammocks of the Keys.
Growth Form: Shrub to small tree.
Similar Species: The leaves of the related Black Ironwood *(Krugiodendron ferreum)* also have blunt or notched apices, but are flexible, not stiff like Darling Plum.
Comments: Darling Plum is listed as a threatened species in Florida.

Red Mangrove
Rhizophora mangle

Plant Family: Rhizophoraceae
Leaves: Opposite, simple, thick, elliptic, to 15 cm, green above, paler green below, appearing whorled at the twig ends.
Bark: Light to medium gray, mottled, with arching reddish-brown prop roots.
Flowers: White to yellow, waxy, with four petals, in sparse clusters in the leaf axils; all year, peaking in the spring.
Fruits: Brown, ovoid, germinating on the tree, the embryonic roots (just beginning in the photo) may reach to over 20 cm long; all year, peaking in summer to fall.
Habitat: Shallow salt water of the coastal zone.
Growth Form: Shrub to small tree, almost always in extensive single species thickets at the seaward edge of the mangrove zone.
Key Features: Of the mangroves, Red Mangrove has leaves green above, paler green below, and reddish-brown prop roots.
Comments: Coastal, at the seaward edge of the mangrove zone; the "walking tree". Generally a small tree in Florida, it may grow much larger further south in the tropics.

Buttonbush
Cephalanthus occidentalis

Plant Family: Rubiaceae

Leaves: Opposite, simple, usually in whorls of 3 (sometimes 4); elliptic, shiny, with long pointed apices, to 16 cm long.

Bark: Brown, fissured; the trunk is narrow.

Flowers: Individually very small and white, but collectively held on long-stalked globular heads that look like pincushions; seen from spring into early summer.

Fruits: The small seeds are found on globular heads from late summer into fall.

Habitat: Buttonbush forms dense, single species thickets along the shores of slow flowing watercourses.

Growth Form: Usually an aquatic shrub with multiple trunks, rarely a small tree.

Key Feature: The large, shiny, elliptic leaves held in whorls of 3 or 4 distinguish Buttonbush from all other aquatic shrubs.

Comments: Buttonbush is a native aquatic shrub that ranges from south Florida, west to Texas, and north to southern Canada and New England. There are disjunct populations in Arizona and California. Bees make a distinctive honey from the blossoms, deer browse on the leaves, and ducks and small mammals eat the seeds.

Black Torch
Erithalis fruticosa

Plant Family: Rubiaceae
Leaves: Opposite, simple, thick, oval to elliptic, to 5 cm, with rounded or blunt-pointed apices.
Bark: Mottled brown and gray, somewhat rough, usually with multiple trunks.
Flowers: Small, white, with five petals (sometimes more), arising in clusters from the leaf axils; the flowers and fruits may appear together; present year round.
Fruits: Rounded, green, in hanging clusters, turning pink and finally ripening to a shiny black, to about 1 cm; eaten by birds and other wildlife; present all year.
Habitat: Coastal hammocks and sandy soils; more common on the Keys.

Growth Form: Commonly a dense shrub with multiple trunks, it may occasionally attain the status of a small tree.
Similar Species: Possibly confused with Spanish Stopper, but the leaves of Black Torch are thick and the flowers lack bushy stamens.
Comments: Black Torch is a West Indian species, which reaches its northernmost distribution in south Florida where it is listed as a threatened species. The resinous wood has been split and used for torches in Caribbean countries.

Princewood
Exostema caribaeum

Plant Family: Rubiaceae

Leaves: Opposite, simple, elliptic, to 8 cm, dark green above, lighter below, re-curved up from the midrib.

Bark: Mottled brown and gray, rough; the twigs are jointed with stipules present.

Flowers: Monoecious, large, white, solitary, tubular, with five petals, held in the leaf axils; mostly late spring to late summer, also at other times of the year.

Fruits: Two part woody capsules seen from summer into late fall.

Habitat: Coastal hammocks of the Keys, occasional on the extreme southern peninsula.

Growth Form: Small tree.

Key Features: The showy flowers, opposite re-curved leaves, and jointed twigs will identify Princewood.

Comments: Princewood is an endangered species that is uncommon in its hammock habitat.

Seven-Year Apple
Genipa clusiifolia

Plant Family: Rubiaceae

Leaves: Opposite, simple, obovate, glossy, with rounded apices, the margins are rolled under, to 15 cm; the leaves tend to cluster at the twig ends; the midribs are thick and cream-colored at the base.

Bark: Light mottled gray or brown, rough to blocky on older specimens.

Flowers: Dioecious, white, with five sharp-pointed petals, found at the twig ends from spring into summer.

Fruits: Green, large and egg-shaped, to 10 cm, held at the twig ends, turning darker and eventually puckering like a prune when ripe. This process takes months, but not seven years! Some people like the taste of the pulp but most do not. The seeds are mildly toxic.

Habitat: Coastal hammocks, beaches, sandy soils; also commonly planted as an ornamental.

Growth Form: A shrub to small tree with very attractive flowers, fruits, and foliage.

Similar Species: Florida Clusea *(Clusia rosea)* has duller green leaves and attains medium tree height, larger than this species.

Comments: In older field guides this species is referenced as *Casasia clusiifolia*.

Everglades Velvetseed
Guettarda elliptica

Plant Family: Rubiaceae

Leaves: Opposite, simple, to 6 cm, the shape varies from ovate to obovate to elliptic, apices pointed or sometimes notched, soft hairy to the touch, the veins curve to follow the leaf edges.

Bark: Light mottled gray, smooth, often with multiple trunks.

Flowers: Small, cream-colored to pink, with four petals, in sparse clusters in the leaf axils; appearing from spring into summer.

Fruits: A green drupe, ripening to red- purple, downy, in flat clusters in the leaf axils, edible, if not palatable, best left to the birds! Seen late summer into fall.

Habitat: Hammocks and pinelands, limestone soils.

Growth Form: A shrub in the pinelands, a small tree in hammocks.

Similar Species: Rough Velvetseed *(Guettarda scabra)* has larger, broadly elliptic, rough-textured leaves, and it attains medium-sized tree height, typically larger than this species.

Comments: Everglades Velvetseed ranges from south Florida through the West Indies to Central and South America.

Rough Velvetseed
Guettarda scabra

Plant Family: Rubiaceae

Leaves: Opposite, simple, broadly ovate to elliptic, with pointed apices, to 15 cm, the leaf veins follow the leaf edges; the leaves feel like fine sandpaper to the touch.

Bark: Light gray, lightly rough, often with multiple trunks.

Flowers: White to pink, short and tubular, with 5 or more petals, held in sparse clusters in the leaf axils; usually spring to summer, but may appear at other times of the year.

Fruits: A red drupe, ripening to black, downy, to 1 cm, held in the leaf axils; typically late summer into fall.

Habitat: Hammock edges and pinelands, including limestone and sandy soils.

Growth Form: Small to medium-sized tree.

Similar Species: Everglades Velvetseed *(Guettarda elliptica)* has smaller, soft-textured leaves, and is a smaller tree.

Comments: Rough Velvetseed ranges from south Florida through the West Indies to Central and South America.

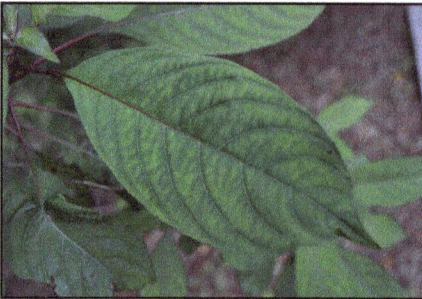

Scarlet Bush
Hamelia patens

Plant Family: Rubiaceae
Leaves: Opposite, simple, but often in whorls of 3 or 4, elliptic, to 18 cm, new leaves and leaf petioles are red. Leaf veins are prominent and follow the leaf edges.
Bark: Brown, rough.
Flowers: Orange-red, tubular, to 5 cm, in attractive terminal clusters; present all year.

Fruits: A round red berry, to 1 cm, ripening to dark purple, edible; throughout the year.
Habitat: Hammock edges, thickets, widely planted.
Growth Form: Usually a shrub, but may take the form of a small tree.
Similar Species: Buttonbush *(Cephalanthus occidentalis)* also has whorled leaves of a similar shape, but is aquatic. The beautiful flowers and fruits of Scarlet Bush, if present, allow for easy identification.

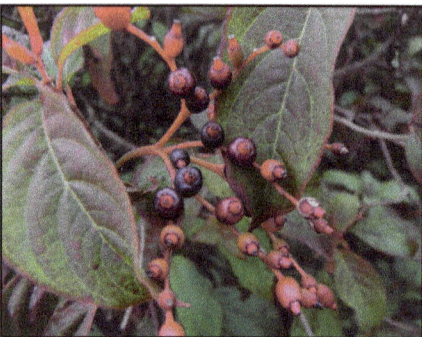

Comments: Scarlet Bush is a widely cultivated south Florida species, the flowers are very attractive to hummingbirds. Scarlet Bush ranges south to Central and South America where extracts of the leaves are used medicinally to treat skin disorders.

Wild Coffee
Psychotria nervosa

Plant Family: Rubiaceae

Leaves: Opposite, simple, elliptic, glossy, bright green, with pointed apices, to 15 cm; the veins are depressed and very prominent.

Bark: Light brown, smooth, with multiple trunks.

Flowers: Small, white, sessile, with 5 petals, in clusters in the leaf axils, they attract insect pollinators; early spring to summer.

Fruits: A dark red drupe, in rounded clusters in the leaf axils, relished by birds; fall to winter.

Habitat: Common in the understory of hammocks and pinelands, it is also widely cultivated for its distinctive leaves.

Growth Form: Usually a shrub, rarely a small tree.

Similar Species: Three other *Psychotria* species are also called Wild Coffee - *P. sulzneri* has leaves that are not glossy; *P. ligustrifolia* has long stalked flower clusters; *P. punctata* has dots on the bottom of the leaves.

Comments: Plants in the genus *Psychotria* are related to the true coffees, but the berries will not yield that popular beverage. Wild Coffee also grows in the West Indies and Central America.

Randia
(White Indigo Berry)
Randia aculeata

Plant Family: Rubiaceae

Leaves: Opposite, simple, obovate to elliptic, to 6 cm, tend to crowd toward the twig ends, sharp stipules may be present where leaf meets twig. The twigs are held at a 45-degree angle off the main stem.

Bark: Gray, rough and blocky on older trees, the branches are often thorny.

Flowers: Dioecious, white, with five petals, fragrant, some appear directly on the branches, others in the leaf axils, at any time of year, peaking in the spring and summer months.

Fruits: A rounded green berry, to 1 cm, ripening to white, with blue-black pulp. The berries were formerly used to make dye and ink; usually fall into winter.

Habitat: Pinelands, sandy soils, hammock edges. Randia is drought resistant and salt tolerant, making it a hardy specimen in coastal plantings.

Growth Form: Shrub to small tree.

Key Features: The combination of small, obovate leaves and the twigs held at a 45-degree angle will distinguish Randia from other opposite leaved species.

Comments: Randia is a variable species, some trees lack leaf stipules or will have larger leaves and fruits.

Red Maple
Acer rubrum

Plant Family: Sapindaceae

Leaves: The familiar maple leaf; opposite, simple, toothed, with 3 to 5 pointed lobes, green above, lighter beneath, to 15 cm, although many leaves are smaller; turning red in the fall.

Bark: Light to dark gray, smooth on younger trees, fissured to blocky on older specimens.

Flowers: Small, red, lacking petals; appearing from winter to early spring before the leaves.

Fruits: The paired seeds with wings are called samaras and are found in spring.

Habitat: Moist to swampy soils, where it may grow quite rapidly.

Growth Form: Small to medium-sized tree.

Similar Species: Red maple is the only maple species found in south Florida.

Comments: Uncommon in the Everglades and not found on the Keys. Red Maple is one of the most widespread trees in eastern North America, ranging from south Florida west to the Mississippi drainage and north into southern Canada and New England. It often grows in pure stands in swamps further north and its presence here is a wonderful example of certain trees with a more northerly distribution that manage to exist in south Florida.

87

Fiddlewood
Citharexylum spinosum

Plant Family: Verbenaceae

Leaves: Opposite, simple, shiny, elliptic, to 15 cm, the veins follow the leaf edges, petioles and midribs may be orange on some specimens. The leaves typically droop downward off the twigs and branches.

Bark: Light gray-brown, the twigs are square.

Flowers: Dioecious, small, white, tubular, with 5 petals, fragrant, in racemes in the leaf axils and at the branch ends; attractive to butterflies; late spring to summer, sometimes at other times of the year.

Fruits: A green drupe that turns bright orange and eventually ripens to black, on long racemes, edible and sweet; usually from late summer into fall.

Habitat: Fairly common in coastal hammocks and pinelands.

Growth Form: Shrub to small tree.

Key Features: Fiddlewood is the only hammock species with long opposite drooping leaves and square twigs.

Comments: The common name comes from the French term for this plant, "bois fidele" which translates as "good wood."

Snowberry, with white flowers and fruits,
is a common vine in south Florida hammocks

Trees with alternate, simple leaves

Mango
Mangifera indica

Plant Family: Anacardiaceae

Leaves: Alternate, simple, long and lanceolate, to 24 cm, midribs and side veins yellowish; the leaf petiole is enlarged at the base.

Bark: Brown to gray, rough or fissured.

Flowers: Small, white to pink or orange, found in long narrow clusters on distinctly red twigs; seen from winter into early spring.

Fruits: A large, ovoid drupe, to 15 cm, ripening to greenish or reddish yellow; spring to summer. The orange pulp is sweet and delicious and is used in recipes worldwide. Plant breeders have produced over 100 different cultivars of this important commercial species.

Habitat: Widely planted, both commercially and in yards and gardens; Mango sometimes naturalizes in coastal areas of south Florida.

Growth Form: A medium-sized densely crowned tree that has a single, straight trunk.

Key Feature: The long lanceolate leaves with conspicuous parallel side veins are unlike any other south Florida tree.

Comments: Mango is native to India, but was long ago introduced into other tropical countries; it is the most commonly cultivated tropical tree on earth, with close to 40 million tons of fruit produced annually!

Pond Apple
Annona glabra

Plant Family: Annonaceae

Leaves: Alternate, simple, leathery, broadly elliptic, shiny green above, paler below, to 13 cm; the leaf edges tend to turn up.

Bark: Gray-brown, blocky to lightly fissured; the trunk is typically short and the base is often buttressed, especially in standing water.

Flowers: The three-part buds give rise to white or light yellow flowers with six petals that are seen from spring into summer.

Fruits: Large, apple-like, to 15 cm long, green, ripening to yellow, edible; late summer to fall, persisting on the tree into winter. The fruit floats and transports the seeds to new habitats.

Habitat: Common in swamps and damp woods throughout the southern peninsula, Pond Apple is never found in drier habitats.

Growth Form: Small to medium-sized tree.

Similar Species: The leaves could be confused with the figs, but the large fruits, if present, are unlike any other swamp-dwelling tree.

Comments: The large fruits are relished by wildlife (even alligators may eat the fruits!). Pond Apple has been introduced to Hawaii and Australia, where it is considered an invasive species.

Dahoon Holly
Ilex cassine

Plant Family: Aquifoliaceae

Leaves: Alternate, simple, oblanceolate to narrowly elliptic, shiny, green above, whitish green below, apices may have a sharp bristle, to 8 cm; some of the leaves may be lightly toothed on the upper margins.

Bark: Light gray, smooth, becoming lightly fissured on older trees.

Flowers: Dioecious, small, white, with 4 petals, either solitary or in short-stalked clusters along the branches from late spring into summer.

Fruits: A stalked green drupe, ripening to an attractive bright red (sometimes yellow), to 1 cm in diameter, borne along the branches of the female trees and persisting for many weeks, starting in the fall. The fruits are attractive to birds and small mammals.

Habitat: Fairly common in wet hammocks, swamps, and wetland edges, yet is drought tolerant once established, for example, in depressions in the pinelands.

Growth Form: A small shrubby tree, often with 2 or 3 narrow trunks.

Similar Species: Tawnyberry Holly *(Ilex krugiana)* also has elliptic leaves, but they usually lack teeth or bristled apices and the fruits ripen to purple-black; it is also uncommon, found only in certain Everglades hammocks.

Comments: Dahoon Holly is found in wetlands throughout Florida, except on the Keys.

Black Calabash
Amphitecna latifolia

Plant Family: Bignoniaceae
Leaves: Alternate, simple, obovate, to 18 cm long, apices are short-pointed.
Bark: Light brown or gray, somewhat rough.
Flowers: Purplish-white, bell-shaped, 5 to 6 cm long, held on short stalks; appearing at any time of the year.
Fruits: Dark green, hard, egg-shaped; they split to reveal dark edible seeds in a whitish pulp.
Habitat: Hammocks of the east coast, also planted as an ornamental.
Growth Form: Small tree with dense foliage.
Key Features: The purplish flowers, hard fruits, and leaves with a short-pointed tip will identify this native species.
Comments: Black Calabash is uncommon in south Florida where it reaches its northernmost distribution; it is more common in Mexico, Central America and the West Indies.

Calabash
Crescentia cujete

Plant Family: Bignoniaceae

Leaves: Alternate, simple, oblanceolate, to 14 cm long, often clustered on short spur branches.

Bark: Brown to gray, smooth on young trees, blocky and fissured on older specimens.

Flowers: Light green with purple markings, bell-shaped, found singly on the older branches; pollinated by bats (a flower bud is shown); appearing all year.

Fruits: Large, rounded, gourd-like, green to brown, up to 30 cm in diameter, found singly on the trunk and older branches.

Habitat: Naturalized in hammocks; grown in yards and gardens as a specimen tree.

Growth Form: Small to medium-sized tree.

Key Features: The flowers and large fruits that grow directly from the trunk and older branches will identify Calabash.

Comments: Calabash is native to Central and South America and has been introduced to India and other tropical countries. The pulp of the fruit is not edible but is used in folk medicine as an anti-inflammatory. The hard outer shell is fashioned into bowls, cups, water containers, and musical instruments.

Bahama Strongbark
Bourreria succulenta

Plant Family: Boraginaceae
Leaves: Alternate, simple, obovate, smooth, to 10 cm, the apices are rounded or may be notched, lighter green beneath. The tree may lose many leaves in the winter dry season (tardily deciduous) but they come back in a robust fashion with the spring and summer rains.
Bark: Red-brown, rough and fissured.
Flowers: Monoecious, white, with 5 rounded petals, bell-shaped, in terminal clusters, found all year, peaking in the summer; they are attractive to bees and butterflies.
Fruits: An orange drupe, to 1 cm, held in flat clusters at the branch ends; they provide food for birds from late summer into winter.
Habitat: Keys hammocks.
Growth Form: Shrub to small tree, the branch ends tend to droop down.
Similar Species: Rough Strongbark *(Bourreira radula)* is a rare Keys species that has shorter leaves that are rough to the touch.
Comments: Bahamian and West Indian women have used the bark to make a tea that is reported to make their men more virile, explaining the common name. Bahama Strongbark is called *Bourreria ovata* in older references.

95

Geiger Tree
Cordia sebestena

Plant Family: Boraginaceae

Leaves: Alternate, simple, broadly ovate, to 25 cm, dark green above, lighter green below, some leaves may be toothed toward the apex; older leaves are rough to the touch, like fine sandpaper.

Bark: Dark gray and fissured, even on young trees; the twigs are green.

Flowers: Orange, with 5 petals, in terminal clusters, quite distinctive, they are attractive to hummingbirds; usually spring to summer, also at other times of the year.

Fruits: A green pear-shaped drupe that ripens to white, with a blunt-pointed apex, to about 4 cm long; reported as edible, but not that palatable; summer to fall.

Habitat: Hammock edges of the Keys; Geiger Tree is not common, although there is a fine station at Bahia Honda State Park, and it is widely planted as an ornamental on the Keys.

Growth Form: Small tree.

Similar Species: Rough Velvetseed *(Guettarda scabra)* also has rough textured leaves, but they are opposite along the stem. The orange flowers of Gieger Tree, if present, allow for easy identification.

Comments: The common name honors John Geiger, a nineteenth century Key West ship captain, and was bestowed by none other than the famous John James Audubon, who stayed with Geiger while painting the birds of the Keys.

96

Cinnamon Bark
(Canella)
Canella winterana

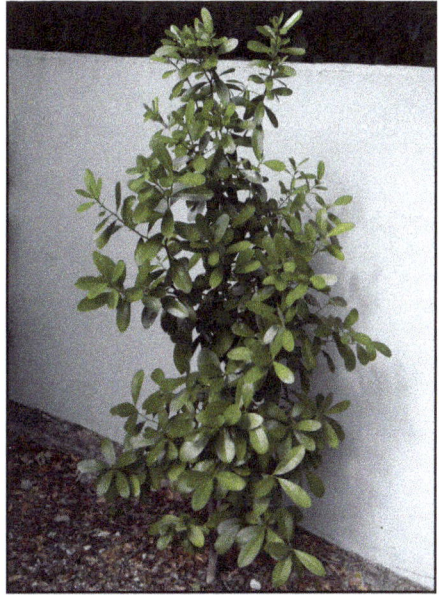

Plant Family: Canellaceae

Leaves: Alternate, simple, obovate, shiny, dark green, to 12 cm, apices are rounded or may be notched; new growth is a lighter green.

Bark: Brown, rough on younger trees, lightly fissured on older specimens; the inner bark is yellow.

Flowers: The buds open to reveal red flowers with five petals, held in short clusters at the branch ends throughout the year, peaking in summer.

Fruits: Green stalked berries, ripening to bright red, found in clusters or singly at the branch ends from winter into spring.

Habitat: Sandy soils, hammock edges of the Keys.

Growth Form: A small, densely shrubby tree with one or two trunks.

Key Features: The obovate leaves, brown bark, and spicy taste of the leaves will identify Canella.

Comments: Canella is Latin for cinnamon, but this is not the same tree that produces commercial cinnamon, which is native to Southeast Asia, although the inner bark has a scent of cinnamon and has been used in the West Indies to produce a pungent spice and medicinal drink.

Southern Hackberry
(Sugarberry)
Celtis laevigata

Plant Family: Cannabaceae

Leaves: Alternate, simple, ovate to lanceolate, with long pointed apices and asymmetrical bases; the margins are often toothed but some leaves lack the teeth, to 15 cm.

Bark: Gray, smooth on young trees, becoming covered with small knob-like protuberances on older trees.

Flowers: Dioecious, small, greenish, in the leaf axils; seen from spring into early summer.

Fruits: A long-stalked drupe that holds a single seed, to about 1 cm in diameter, green, ripening to reddish purple, found in the leaf axils from late summer into fall.

Habitat: Hammock edges on dry or wet soils; not found on the Keys.

Growth Form: Small to large tree.

Key Features: The long-pointed leaves with uneven bases, combined with the rough gray bark will identify Southern Hackberry.

Comments: The fruits (sugarberries) are sought by wildlife for their high energy content.

Florida Trema
Trema micrantha

Plant Family: Cannabaceae

Leaves: Alternate, simple, broadly ovate, with pointed apices, the margins are finely toothed, to 15 cm; distinctly rough to the touch on the top surface, like fine sandpaper. The leaves are held on the branches in a flattened two-ranked arrangement.

Bark: Light brown, rough, with small lenticels.

Flowers: Dioecious, small, greenish, in the leaf axils; appearing spring to summer for established trees, but at any time of year for younger trees.

Fruits: Small bright orange drupes that are found in the leaf axils; from fall into winter, but at other times of the year for younger trees.

Habitat: Florida Trema is a common pioneer species that colonizes open sunlit sites, including hammock edges, roadsides, and other disturbed areas.

Growth Form: Shrub to small tree.

Similar Species: West Indian Trema *(Trema lamarckiana)* also has two-ranked leaves, but they are much smaller, to only 6 cm, and feel rough on both the top and bottom surfaces.

Comments: Florida Trema is the most common of three *Trema* species found in south Florida.

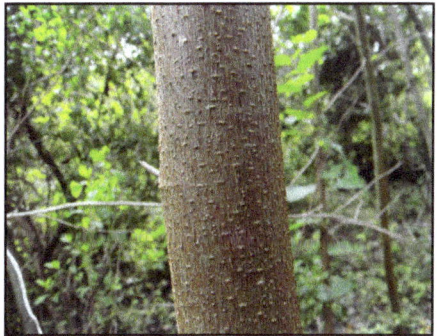

Jamaica Caper
Capparis cynophallophora

Plant Family: Capparaceae

Leaves: Alternate, simple, oblong, to 12 cm, with blunt or notched apices, shiny green above, pale and scaly below.

Bark: Brown to reddish brown and lightly rough or fissured.

Flowers: White, turning purple, with 4 petals and very long stamens, found in loose clusters at the ends of the branches, very fragrant; all year, peaking in spring and summer. The flowers are short-lived, lasting just a day or two and are pollinated by night flying moths.

Fruits: A long tan-colored pod to 25 cm, when ripe it opens to reveal purple seeds in a bright red pulp; all year, peaking summer to fall.

Habitat: Hammock understory near the coast and in sandy soils; it is also planted as an ornamental for its attractive foliage; it is most common on the Keys.

Growth Form: Shrub to small tree.

Similar Species: Bay-leaved Caper *(Capparis flexuosa)* is similar but the leaf undersides are green and the stamens are more numerous.

Comments: The genus *Capparis* includes *C. spinosa*, a European species whose flower buds are the capers used as a condiment.

Limber Caper
(Bay-leaved Caper)
Capparis flexuosa

Plant Family: Capparaceae
Leaves: Alternate, simple, obovate to elliptic, to 12 cm, with blunt or notched apices, green above, lighter green below.
Bark: Mottled gray, smooth.
Flowers: White, turning purple, with 4 petals and very long stamens, found in loose clusters at the ends of the branches; all year, peaking in spring and summer. The flowers are very fragrant but short-lived, lasting just a day or two, and are pollinated by night flying moths.
Fruits: Brown pods to 15 cm that open to reveal white seeds in a scarlet pulp; any time of year, peaking summer to fall.
Habitat: Found in the understory of hammocks near the coast, and in sandy soils.
Growth Form: Shrub to woody vine, a small tree when growing in the sun.
Similar Species: The leaves of Jamaica Caper *(Capparis cynophallophora)* are shiny green above, light silver or light brown below.
Comments: Limber Caper will attain tree status in the sun; it is more commonly found in the shady understory of hammocks where its vine-like growth habit is a good identifying characteristic.

Papaya
Carica papaya

Plant Family: Caricaceae

Leaves: Alternate, simple, very large, to 60 cm, with 7 to 9 long pointed lobes and very long dark purple petioles; the leaves are always held at the top of the trunk; the upper leaf surface is darker than the lower surface.

Bark: Fairly smooth, brown, with large shield-shaped leaf scars.

Flowers: Dioecious, yellow to white, star-shaped, with 5 petals, found in clusters at the leaf bases throughout the year.

Fruits: The well-known papaya; large, to 40 cm or more in diameter, green, ripening to yellow or orange, quite edible and delicious; there are many different cultivars. The black, spicy seeds are edible and can be ground and used as a pepper substitute.

Habitat: Hammock edges, disturbed sites of south Florida and the Keys; its range also extends up both coasts of the peninsula.

Growth Form: Small, short-lived tree with a single, narrow, straight trunk.

Similar Species: Papaya will not be confused with any other Florida tree.

Comments: Papaya originated in Mexico and Central America; it has been introduced as a major commercial crop in tropical regions worldwide.

Coco-plum
Chrysobalanus icaco

Plant Family: Chrysobalanaceae

Leaves: Alternate, simple, glossy, oval to round, the apices are often notched, to 8 cm; held in an upright two-ranked arrangement along the branches.

Bark: Light gray or brown, rough.

Flowers: Small, white, five petals, in small clusters near the branch ends; all year.

Fruits: A purple drupe (the color may vary to a light yellow), to 4 cm, enclosing a single seed; the fruit and its enclosed seed are both edible, and the fruit is used to make preserves in South America.

Habitat: Coco-plum is found in a variety of habitats, frequently near water, and it tends to form thickets in damp soils; it is also widely planted and is sometimes trimmed to form hedges.

Growth Form: Shrub to small tree.

Key Feature: Coco-plum is best identified by its distinctive leaves, which are oval to round and held in two upright ranks along the branches.

Comments: This is a common South Florida species that ranges south into the tropics. The seeds are transported by birds, which love the fruit, and may also be delivered by water to new habitats, explaining its widespread distribution.

Key Lime
Citrus aurantifolia

Plant Family: Citrus (Rutaceae)

Leaves: Alternate, simple, elliptic to ovate, to 10 cm, the petioles are winged, the leaves (like other south Florida trees) may have yellow highlights in the winter dry season.

Bark: Light brown, the branches are quite thorny.

Flowers: White and tinged with purple, with five petals; typically summer, sometimes at other times of the year.

Fruits: Green, turning yellow when ripe; wonderfully juicy and delicious; fall into winter.

Habitat: Planted throughout coastal south Florida, and especially on the Keys, Key Lime is well naturalized.

Growth Form: Shrub to small tree.

Similar Species: The Citrus family consists of many cultivated varieties that hybridize both in nature and as a result of the work of plant breeders (these include grapefruit, orange, tangerine, and others). Complete coverage of these hybrids is beyond the scope of this book.

Comments: Key Lime is a shrubby, thorny tree from Southeast Asia and is widely planted; the fruit is the famous Key Lime, which is especially tart and juicy. A mature well-cared for specimen will produce many fruits.

Buttonwood
Conocarpus erectus

Plant Family: Combretaceae

Leaves: Alternate, simple, stiff, narrowly elliptic, to 10 cm, the terminal twigs and leaf petioles are greenish yellow. Two small glands are on the petiole near the leaf base.

Bark: Dark gray or brown; strongly fissured.

Flowers: Dioecious, greenish white, without petals, in long clusters at the branch ends and in the leaf axils; spring to summer, also at other times of the year.

Fruits: Round brown cones, to 3 cm, that hold small seeds, found in long-stalked clusters that persist for many months.

Habitat: Coastal, typically found inland of the mangroves, but it is salt tolerant and may share habitat with them.

Growth Form: Medium-sized tree, the trunk is usually upright but may lie prostrate and give rise to secondary upright trunks.

Similar Species: Silver Buttonwood *(Conocarpus erectus* var. *sericeus)* is a subspecies that has silvery-gray leaves, but otherwise the same features. It is most often found as an ornamental.

Comments: This hardy tree is a common component of Florida's coastal flora; it is also native to the West Indies, Central and South America, and West Africa.

105

Groundsel Tree
(Saltbush)
Baccharis halimifolia

Plant Family: Compositae (Astera-ceae)

Leaves: Alternate, simple, thick, wedge-shaped, with a few coarse teeth towards the apex, to 8 cm, the terminal leaves may be smaller and lack teeth.

Bark: Gray, fissured on older trees; the twigs are green and distinctly ridged.

Flowers: Dioecious, small, male flowers yellowish, female flowers greenish-white; appearing late summer to fall.

Fruits: The seeds are borne in showy, cottony tufts on the female plants from fall into winter.

Habitat: Typically found in wet coastal areas in various soil types, its range extends inland on disturbed sites and along roads.

Growth Form: Shrub to small tree.

Key Features: The rather unique leaf shape and the ridged twigs should be enough to identify this common species.

Comments: The Composite family is a very successful group of plants, comprising thousands of species; most (such as the asters and daisies) are herbaceous. Groundsel Tree is one of the few plants in this family that has woody stems. This hardy and salt-tolerant tree ranges west to Texas and north along the coastal plain to Massachusetts.

Staggerbush
Lyonia fruticosa

Plant Family: Ericaceae
Leaves: Alternate, simple, elliptic to obovate, with apices rounded or blunt pointed, to 8 cm; green above, paler beneath, new leaves and stems covered with fine rust-colored hairs and this is a good identifying feature.

Bark: Red-brown, smooth on young trees, peeling in short strips on older specimens.

Flowers: Small, white, bell shaped, held in short clusters in the leaf axils, closely resembling those of Blueberry, which is also in the family Ericaceae; seen from spring into summer.

Fruits: Small five-part capsules; summer to fall, but often staying on the tree well into winter.

Habitat: Pinelands

Growth Form: Usually a shrub, rarely a small tree.

Similar Species: *Lyonia ferruginea* is very similar but is more common in central Florida.

Comments: Members of the genus *Lyonia* possess toxic compounds that cause muscle weakness in cattle that browse on the leaves, explaining the common name.

Crabwood
Gymnanthes lucida

Plant Family: Euphorbiaceae
Leaves: Alternate, simple, elliptic to obovate, glossy, to 10 cm, apices may be rounded or come to a blunt point, the margins may be very lightly toothed; the leaf petioles are shouldered where they attach to the twig. Dots of gray or white lichens will often be found growing on some of the leaves.
Bark: Light mottled gray to brown with whitish lenticels.
Flowers: Monoecious, yellow, held on short terminal spikes; forming as buds in summer, they open in spring of the following year.
Fruits: A round capsule, to 1 cm, green, turning brown when mature; late spring to summer.
Habitat: Common in coastal Keys hammocks, uncommon further north.
Growth Form: Shrub to small tree.
Key Feature: The shouldered leaf bases that grasp the stem, lightly toothed leaf margins, and the presence of dot-like lichens on some of the leaves will help identify this common Keys hammock species.
Comments: Crabwood ranges to the Bahamas, the West Indies, and coastal Mexico and Central America. Older field guides reference Crabwood as *Ateramnus lucidus*.

Manchineel
Hippomane mancinella

Plant Family: Euphorbiaceae

Leaves: Alternate, simple, ovate, to 10 cm, the margins may be lightly toothed, the petioles are long and yellow-green, as is the leaf midrib.

Bark: Brown to light gray, fairly smooth on young trees, lightly fissured on older trees.

Flowers: Monoecious, quite small, light green, in long terminal spikes, the female flowers are somewhat larger than the male flowers; seen in spring.

Fruits: A yellow-green drupe, to 5 cm, not unlike a green apple in appearance; summer to fall, but may persist on the tree for several months.

Habitat: Coastal, in moist habitats at the landward edge of the mangrove zone.

Growth Form: Small to medium-sized tree.

Similar Species: The leaves strongly resemble those of the figs (*Ficus* spp.) in size and shape, but the flowers, fruits, and bark are not similar.

Comments: The milky white sap of Manchineel is poisonous, producing severe skin irritation; the fruit is likewise poisonous if ingested, causing throat and esophageal burning. It has thus been persecuted by people, and is now considered endangered in Florida. Look but don't touch!

Chapman Oak
Quercus chapmanii

Plant Family: Fagaceae
Leaves: Alternate, simple, stiff, to 9 cm, quite variable in shape; elliptic to obovate, shiny dark green above, whitish green below, the leaf edges are often wavy and some leaves will have shallow lobes, especially towards the apex.
Bark: Light to medium gray, smooth on young trees, with small blocky plates on older specimens, the twigs are light brown and hairy.
Flowers: Monoecious, male flowers in hanging catkins, female flowers tiny, held in pairs along the twigs from late winter into spring.
Fruits: Small brown sessile acorns, to about 2 cm, the cup covers about one-third of the seed; summer to fall.

Habitat: Pinelands, coastal scrub, sandy soils, throughout Florida and ranging north on the coastal plain to South Carolina.
Growth Form: Shrub to small tree.
Similar Species: Myrtle Oak *(Quercus myrtifolia)*, in the same habitat, has leaves that are green beneath (not whitish green) with the leaf edges always rolled under.
Comments: The state of Florida has about twenty five species of oak, seven are found in south Florida.

Sand Live Oak
Quercus geminata

Plant Family: Fagaceae

Leaves: Alternate, simple, narrowly elliptic, leathery, shiny dark green, with noticeably depressed veins, downy gray below, to 12 cm, but many leaves much shorter; the leaf margins are strongly rolled under.

Bark: Gray-brown, deeply fissured.

Flowers: Monoecious, male flowers in hanging catkins, female flowers tiny, held singly or in pairs along the twigs in the spring.

Fruits: Small, stalked, dark brown to black acorns, to 2.5 cm, with a short cup, covering about one-fourth of the seed, held singly or doubly along the twigs; summer to fall.

Habitat: Dunes, coastal scrub, pinelands and sandy soils, where it tends to form thickets.

Growth Form: Shrub to small tree.

Similar Species: Live Oak *(Quercus virginiana)* has leaf margins that do not roll under and is a much larger tree when mature.

Comments: Sand Live Oak occurs throughout Florida and west along the coast to Louisiana and north to North Carolina. It is highly drought tolerant once established.

111

Darlington Oak
Quercus hemisphaerica

Plant Family: Fagaceae

Leaves: Alternate, simple, narrowly elliptic, to 10 cm, green above, lighter below, some leaves may have sparse teeth toward the apex.

Bark: Gray, lightly fissured on older trees, the twigs are light brown.

Flowers: Monoecious, male flowers in hanging catkins, female flowers tiny; seen in spring.

Fruits: Short light brown acorns, to 1.5 cm, with a short cup; provide food for wildlife; summer to fall.

Habitat: This fast-growing tree is common in oak-pine woods, drier soils, and disturbed sites throughout Florida.

Growth Form: Medium-sized to large tree.

Similar Species: Laurel Oak *(Quercus laurifolia)* is a wetland tree that always has some leaves with a diamond shape.

Comments: Darlington Oak is a relatively short-lived but ecologically important tree. Woodpeckers and small mammals nest in the trunk cavities; insects that inhabit the decaying trunk are the base of the food chain that feed small birds and lizards, which in turn, feed higher order predators like hawks and bobcats.

112

Turkey Oak
Quercus laevis

Plant Family: Fagaceae

Leaves: Alternate, simple, shiny, dark green above, a bit lighter beneath, up to 25 cm, but most leaves are shorter. Some leaves are 3-lobed and look like turkey tracks; most leaves have 5 to 7 deeply incised lobes with bristles at the tips, similar to the northern Scarlet Oak.

Bark: Medium to dark gray, blocky on older trees, the twigs are a lighter gray.

Flowers: Monoecious, male flowers in long hanging catkins near the branch ends that emerge in spring along with the young leaves; female flowers inconspicuous.

Fruits: Brown acorns, to 2.5 cm, with a prominent scaly cup that covers about one-third to one-half of the seed; summer to fall.

Habitat: Pinelands and dry sandy soils where it may form pure stands; it is also planted in state parks.

Growth Form: Shrub to a potentially medium-sized tree.

Key Feature: The deeply incised leaves are turned sideways to avoid the heat of direct sunlight during the middle of the day.

Comments: Turkey Oak is a coastal plain tree that ranges west to Louisiana and north to the Carolinas. It is highly drought tolerant and produces numerous acorns important to wildlife.

113

Laurel Oak
(Diamond Leaf Oak)
Quercus laurifolia

Plant Family: Fagaceae
Leaves: Alternate, simple, obovate, to 10 cm, fairly glossy and smooth, edges often wavy, the apices are blunt pointed and at least some leaves have a diamond-shaped (rhomboid) form.
Bark: Dark gray, rough and fissured; the trunks of mature specimens are often buttressed at the base, especially near water.
Flowers: Monoecious, male flowers in hanging catkins, female flowers inconspicuous along the twigs; from spring into summer.
Fruits: A brown acorn, to 2 cm, with a short cup; fall to winter.
Habitat: Swamps, low wet woodlands, and other damp situations.
Growth Form: A medium-sized to large tree.
Similar Species: The wet habitat, combined with the presence of some diamond-shaped leaves on any tree will distinguish it from Darlington Oak *(Quercus hemisphaerica)*.
Comments: Laurel Oak is a common species in its favored wetland habitat; it is not found on the Keys. Its range tends to overlap that of its relative Live Oak *(Quercus virginiana)*.

Myrtle Oak
Quercus myrtifolia

Plant Family: Fagaceae

Leaves: Alternate, simple, obovate to oval, small, to 8 cm, the top surface is shiny and dark green, lighter green and lacking hairs beneath, the leaf edges are turned under, the apices are rounded.

Bark: Gray to brown, fairly smooth for an oak, rougher on older trees, the twigs are light brown.

Flowers: Monoecious, male flowers in hanging catkins that appear in spring, female flowers inconspicuous along the twigs.

Fruits: A dark brown stalked acorn, to 2 cm, with a short cup that covers less than one-half of the seed; held singly or in pairs along the branches from summer into fall.

Habitat: Myrtle Oak is a coastal tree that is found in pinelands and sandy scrub where it tends to form thickets.

Growth Form: Shrub to small tree.

Similar Species: Chapman Oak *(Quercus chapmanii)*, found in the same habitat, has leaves that are whitish-green beneath and leaf edges not rolled under.

Comments: Myrtle Oak shares habitat with Chapman Oak and Sand Live Oak, and they are collectively called scrub oaks. In the northern counties of south Florida they make up the understory of the Sand Pine scrub community.

Live Oak
Quercus virginiana

Plant Family: Fagaceae

Leaves: Alternate, simple, elliptic, stiff, to 12 cm, but many leaves are shorter, dark green above, light gray and downy below.

Bark: Brown-gray, fissured, holding a wide variety of epiphytes on mature trees.

Flowers: Monoecious, small, the male flowers are in hanging terminal catkins, the female flowers are not conspicuous and are further back on the stems.

Fruits: A blackish acorn, to 2.5 cm, with a short cup that covers less than one-half of the seed.

Habitat: Uplands and drier habitats throughout Florida, it is the only Florida oak that occurs on the Keys.

Growth Form: Large tree.

Similar Species: Sand Live Oak (*Quercus geminata)* has leaf margins rolled under, the leaf veins strongly depressed, and it is a much smaller tree when mature.

Comments: In the open Live Oak is an impressively large, long-lived, short-trunked tree with many spreading branches. Its range includes the coastal plain of the Deep South, west to Texas.

116

Lancewood
Ocotea coriacea

Plant Family: Lauraceae
Leaves: Alternate, simple, lanceolate to narrowly elliptic, apices sharp pointed or sometimes blunt pointed; dark green above, lighter green below, to 15 cm, fragrant when crushed, the petioles have a distinctive J or S shape and this is a good field mark.
Bark: Light gray, smooth, becoming darker reddish brown and furrowed with age.
Flowers: Small, white, with 4 to 6 petals, found in clusters in the leaf axils from spring into summer.
Fruits: A green drupe, ripening to dark blue, to 1 cm, held on bright red stalks; fall to winter.
Habitat: A common species in coastal hammocks and pinelands.
Growth Form: Often shrubby, Lancewood also attains small tree status.
Similar Species: Red Bay *(Persea borbonia)* has light gray leaf undersides. Guiana Plum *(Drypetes lateriflora)* has crushed leaves that are not fragrant and has red fruits.
Comments: The range of Lancewood includes the Bahamas, the West Indies, and the eastern coast of Central America. Lancewood was formerly classified as *Nectandria coriacea*.

Avocado
Persea americana

Plant Family: Lauraceae

Leaves: Alternate, simple, stiff, glossy, dark green, broadly elliptic, to 30 cm, tend to crowd toward the branch ends.

Bark: Brown, fissured, new twigs are green.

Flowers: Green to cream-colored, somewhat showy, stamens yellow, in terminal clusters from late winter into spring.

Fruits: Pear-shaped, fleshy, large, to 18 cm, edible; the color can be green to yellow-green to purple depending on the cultivar. The single seed is large and rounded. Like the banana, Avocado will only ripen after it is picked.

Habitat: Avocado is widely cultivated and does well in most well-drained soil types, it occasionally naturalizes.

Growth Form: Small to medium-sized tree.

Key Features: The large pear-shaped fruits and large, broadly elliptic leaves will identify Avocado.

Comments: Avocado is native to Mexico but has been introduced into tropical and warm-temperate countries around the world. The common name is derived from the Aztec word for the fruit. Avocado has one of the highest energy contents of any fruit; it is rich in unsaturated fat and has many culinary uses.

Red Bay
Persea borbonia

Plant Family: Lauraceae

Leaves: Alternate, simple, lanceolate to narrowly elliptic, the leaves are aromatic when crushed, to 15 cm, green above, grayish white below.

Bark: Gray-brown, becoming darker and furrowed with age.

Flowers: Small, light greenish yellow, in clusters in the leaf axils; appearing from spring into summer.

Fruits: A distinctly stalked drupe, to 1 cm, green, ripening to blue; seen from late summer into fall; reportedly browsed by deer and turkey.

Habitat: A rather common Florida tree that is found in various habitats, including marsh edges, hammocks, and sandy soils, it ranges west on the coastal plain to Texas and north to Virginia.

Growth Form: Small to medium-sized tree.

Similar Species: Lancewood *(Ocotea coriacea)* has green leaf undersides; Swamp Bay *(Persea palustris)* has leaves brown-hairy beneath, especially along the midrib, and grows in wetter areas.

Comments: The presence of leaf galls caused by insects, and the resulting sickle-shaped leaves is diagnostic. More problematic has been the recent introduction of a small Asian beetle that vectors a fungal disease (Laurel Wilt) that has been killing Red Bay throughout its range.

Silk Bay
Persea humilus

Plant Family: Lauraceae
Leaves: Alternate, simple, lanceolate to narrowly elliptic, the leaves are aromatic when crushed, to 10 cm, shiny dark green above, light gray to brown and silky beneath.
Bark: Light brown on young trees, turning dark brown to blackish and rougher on older trees.
Flowers: Small, light greenish yellow, in clusters in the leaf axils; spring to summer.
Fruits: A distinctly stalked drupe, to 1 cm, green, ripening to blue-black; late summer to fall.
Habitat: Silk Bay is most common in the dry, sand pine scrub of central Florida; it is not as common in south Florida.
Growth Form: Small to medium-sized tree.
Key Feature: The light gray to brown, hairy leaf undersides will separate Silk Bay from the other *Persea* species.
Comments: All of the *Persea* species, except the cultivated Avocado, are larval host plants for the Spicebush Swallowtail butterfly.

Swamp Bay
Persea palustris

Plant Family: Lauraceae
Leaves: Alternate, simple, lanceolate to elliptic, shiny, the leaves are aromatic when crushed, to 15 cm, green above, light green below, brown hairy along the midrib.
Bark: Gray to brown with white lenticels, becoming dark reddish brown and furrowed with age, the twigs and buds are brown-hairy.
Flowers: Small, light greenish yellow, in stalked clusters in the leaf axils; spring to summer.
Fruits: A stalked drupe, to 1 cm, green, ripening to blue; from late summer into fall.
Habitat: Swamps, marsh edges, and along canals, wherever water is present.
Growth Form: Small tree.
Similar Species: Lancewood *(Ocotea coriacea)* has green leaf undersides, Red Bay *(Persea borbonia)* has light gray leaf undersides, lacks brown-hairy twigs, and tends to grow in drier habitats.
Comments: The presence of leaf galls caused by insects, and the resulting sickle-shaped leaves, is diagnostic. The leaves of Swamp Bay, Silk Bay, and Red Bay can be used to make tea, and as a culinary substitute for the spice Bayleaf, a European species from the same family.

Earleaf Acacia
Acacia auriculiformis

Plant Family: Leguminosae
Leaves: Alternate, simple, narrow, often curved, to 15 cm; the veins run parallel to the leaf margins.

Bark: Brown to gray, fairly smooth when young, becoming rough and lightly fissured on older trees.

Flowers: Bright yellow, individually small but held on spikes up to 8 cm long that arise from the leaf axils in late winter to spring.

Fruits: A flattened, twisted, dark brown pod, to 8 cm, that holds black seeds; typically seen from summer into fall.

Habitat: This fast-growing, non-native tree is found in a variety of habitats, from sand pine scrub to hammocks; it also tolerates wetland soils.

Growth Form: Small to medium-sized tree with a crooked, gnarled appearance.

Key Features: The distinctive leaf shape, and the yellow spike of flowers, will identify this weedy tree.

Comments: Earleaf Acacia is native to tropical Australia, Indonesia and New Guinea; it is planted in other tropical countries, primarily for fuel wood and paper pulp, and to recolonize waste sites. It tolerates a wide range of soil pH, and like other legumes, the root nodules fix nitrogen in the soil. It is listed as a Class I invasive species in Florida.

Orchid Tree
Bauhinia variegata

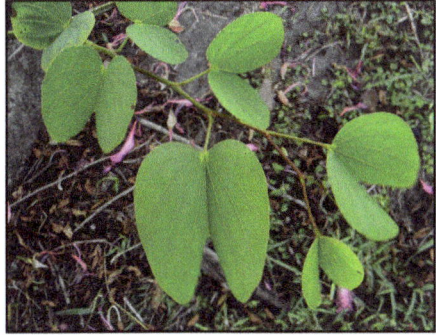

Plant Family: Leguminosae

Leaves: Alternate, simple, two lobed, to 15 cm, the apices are deeply notched, resulting in a very distinctive shape.

Bark: Gray and smooth on younger trees, rougher on older trees.

Flowers: Large, fragrant, red-purple, with five petals, incredibly showy, some cultivars are white; late winter to spring.

Fruits: A flat pod, to 20 cm long; summer to fall.

Habitat: Orchid Tree will typically be found in plantings in town and city parks and on private land, but it has spread to the wild and is invasive in south Florida in hammock margins and pine rocklands.

Growth Form: Small to medium-sized tree.

Key Features: The combination of showy flowers and the unusual leaf shape will distinguish the Bauhinia species from all other south Florida trees.

Comments: Orchid Tree is native to Southeast Asia; it is the most common of a few similar *Bauhinia* species that are grown in south Florida.

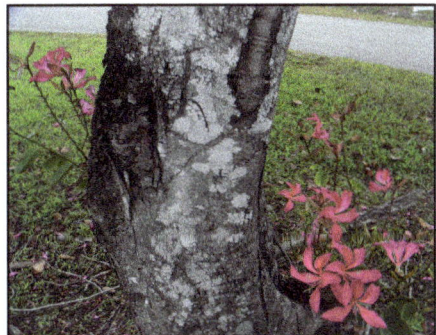

Sweetbay Magnolia
Magnolia virginiana

Plant Family: Magnoliaceae
Leaves: Alternate, simple, narrowly elliptic, appearing whorled at the twig ends, to 15 cm, somewhat leathery, green above, whitish below. The crushed leaves have a spicy scent.
Bark: Light gray, smooth, darker and rougher on older trees.
Flowers: The familiar magnolia flower, white, large, fragrant and showy, to 8 cm in diameter, the fragrance is lemony (a flower bud is shown); spring to early summer.
Fruits: Aggregate, egg-shaped, green, ripening to dark red, to 8 cm, the fruits enclose black seeds with a bright red fleshy covering that are eaten by birds; late summer into winter.
Habitat: Swamps, wet hammocks, and other moist situations.
Growth Form: Small to medium-sized tree.
Key Features: The narrowly elliptic leaves are whitish beneath. That feature, combined with the flowers or fruits, if present, should separate it from other trees with alternate leaves.
Comments: Sweetbay Magnolia ranges north to the Delmarva Peninsula and west across the Deep South to east Texas.

Wild Cotton
Gossypium hirsutum

Plant Family: Malvaceae

Leaves: Alternate, simple, 3-lobed, with very long petioles, to 15 cm.

Bark: Light brown, with single or multiple trunks.

Flowers: Cream-colored, large and attractive, each petal has a red spot at the base; any time of year.

Fruits: A brown triangular capsule that splits to reveal the cottony seeds; present year-round.

Habitat: Rare in hammock edges, thickets, and disturbed sites, much more common in cultivation in south Florida and in tropical regions around the world.

Growth Form: Shrub to small tree.

Similar Species: The related Seaside Mahoe *(Thespesia populnia)* has similar showy flowers, but the leaves are heart-shaped and without lobes.

Comments: Wild Cotton is an endangered species, a victim of a past misguided USDA eradication program designed to protect commercial cotton crops from an insect pest; an effort that practically wiped it out in the wild. Wild Cotton has especially attractive flowers and does well in cultivation.

Seaside Mahoe
(Portia Tree)
Thespesia populnea

Plant Family: Malvaceae

Leaves: Alternate, simple, heart-shaped, to 22 cm, the major veins are yellow and number 5 to 7.

Bark: Gray, strongly fissured on older trees, less so on younger trees.

Flowers: White, with five petals that have a red spot at the base, attractive, to 8 cm across; all year, peaking in summer.

Fruits: Green-yellow, rounded, in five parts, ripening to purple-black, to 5 cm in diameter, they will stay on the tree for some time after ripening.

Habitat: Beaches and thickets along the landward zone of mangrove habitats; this coastal Asian tree is considered an invasive species in south Florida.

Growth Form: A small to medium-sized coastal tree that may attain a wide trunk diameter on older specimens.

Key Features: The coastal habitat, heart-shaped leaves, and distinctive flowers and fruits will identify Seaside Mahoe.

Comments: Seaside Mahoe is important to Indonesian and Pacific Islanders in its native habitat; the wood is carved into tools, ropes are twisted from the inner bark, and the plant provides food and medicine.

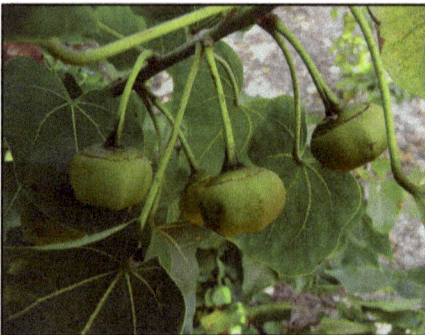

126

False Banyan Tree
Ficus altissima

Plant Family: Moraceae

Leaves: : Alternate, simple, oval to broadly elliptic, shiny, leathery, to 30 cm, apices pointed, petioles and midribs whitish yellow; the first pair of veins form an obvious V.

Bark: Gray to brown, smooth; aerial roots that reach the ground become woody trunks, forming a dense lattice that may extend over a large area.

Flowers: Minute, found within the fruit.

Fruits: Yellow to red, held in the leaf axils, without a stalk, 2 cm in diameter; inside will be found the many miniscule flowers, which are pollinated by a tiny wasp; through-out the year, peaking in spring and summer.

Habitat: Hammocks, and grow-ing as a street tree.

Growth Form: Large tree.

Similar Species: The 90 degree V-shape of the first pair of veins from the midrib will separate False Banyan Tree from native *Ficus* spe-cies. The pointed leaf apices will separate it from Banyan Tree *(Ficus benghalensis)*.

Comments: False Banyan is native to India, China, and the Southeast Asian tropics. Due to its invasive nature it is no longer planted as a landscape tree.

127

Strangler Fig
Ficus aurea

Plant Family: Moraceae
Leaves: Alternate, simple, broadly elliptic, shiny, leathery, to 15 cm, leaf petioles and midribs yellow or cream-colored. The twigs end in a pointed green stipule; the sap of broken leaves is white.
Bark: Gray, aerial roots that reach the ground become woody trunks and prop roots, though not to as great an extent as Banyan Tree *(Ficus benghalensis)*.
Flowers: Minute, found within the fruit.
Fruits: Yellow-green, turning to dark red, in the leaf axils, without a stalk, to 2.5 cm, inside will be found the many miniscule flowers which are pollinated by a tiny wasp in a mutualistic relationship with the tree; seen all year, peaking in spring and summer.
Habitat: Hammocks and swamps.
Growth Form: Large tree.
Similar Species: Shortleaf Fig *(Ficus citrifolia)* has stalked fruits and longer leaf petioles.
Comments: Strangler Fig starts as an epiphyte that ultimately strangles and kills the host tree; the fruits are an important food for birds and small mammals.

Banyan Tree
Ficus benghalensis

Plant Family: Moraceae
Leaves: Alternate, simple, broadly ovate, shiny, leathery, to 30 cm, base and apex rounded, petioles and midribs whitish yellow; the first pair of veins from the midrib form an obvious V.

Bark: Gray to brown, smooth; aerial roots that reach the ground become woody trunks, forming a dense lattice that may extend over a large area.

Flowers: Minute, found within the fruit.

Fruits: Orange to red, downy, held in the leaf axils, without a stalk, 2.5 cm in diameter; inside will be found the many miniscule flowers which are pollinated by a tiny wasp; seen all year, peaking in the fall.

Habitat: Hammocks, but mostly planted as a street tree.

Growth Form: Large tree.

Similar Species: The 90 degree V-shape of the first pair of veins from the midrib, and the downy fruits will separate Banyan Tree from native *Ficus* species. The rounded leaf apices will separate it from False Banyan Tree (*Ficus altissima*).

Comments: Banyan Tree is native to India, where it is considered sacred, often sheltering Hindu temples, or acting as a shady retreat for townspeople. It has the broadest canopy spread of any tree, sometimes covering an acre or more!

Shortleaf Fig
Ficus citrifolia

Plant Family: Moraceae

Leaves: Alternate, simple, leathery, with long petioles, to 15 cm, the petioles and midribs are yellow.

Bark: Gray to brown, the trunk is buttressed; thin aerial roots may extend from the trunk and branches.

Flowers: Minute, found within the fruit.

Fruits: Yellow turning to red, on stalks, rounded, to about 2.5 cm; the tiny flowers are inside the fruit and are pollinated by a small wasp that enters by a small hole; all year, peaking in the fall.

Habitat: Hammocks, but almost anywhere a bird drops the seed.

Growth Form: Large tree.

Similar Species: Strangler Fig *(Ficus aurea)* has fruits that lack a stalk and shorter leaf petioles.

Comments: Shortleaf Fig is less likely than Strangler Fig to start as an epiphyte or to produce thick aerial roots. The fruits are an important food for birds and small mammals that act to distribute the seeds via their droppings.

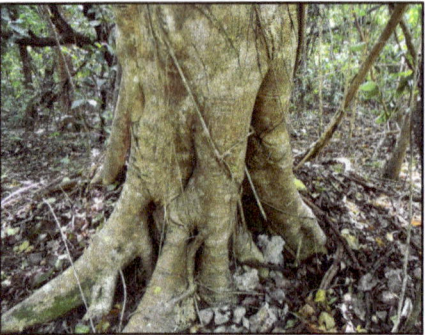

Red Mulberry
Morus rubra

Plant Family: Moraceae
Leaves: Alternate, simple, rough to the touch, margins toothed, to 20 cm, variable in shape, broadly ovate to heart-shaped, or with 2 or 3 lobes; broken petioles reveal a milky sap.
Bark: Gray, lightly fissured.
Flowers: Dioecious (sometimes monoecious), greenish yellow, the male flowers are in hanging catkins up to 5 cm long, the female flowers are in shorter catkins; appearing late spring.
Fruits: Cylindrical clusters up to 3 cm long, red, ripening to purple-black, resembling long blackberries, edible; summer to fall.
Habitat: Variable; typically an understory tree in hammocks and low, wet woods, sometimes found in drier habitats such as pinelands.
Growth Form: Small to medium-sized tree.
Similar Species: The non-native White Mulberry *(Morus alba)* has similar leaves that are smooth to the touch, but is uncommon in south Florida.
Comments: Red Mulberry ranges from Florida west to Texas and north to Ontario and New England. The fruits are attractive to birds and wildlife and are used to make jellies and wine.

Southern Bayberry
(Wax Myrtle)
Myrica cerifera

Plant Family: Myricaceae

Leaves: Alternate, simple, narrowly elliptic, to 15 cm, often toothed (sometimes not) toward the apex, aromatic; tiny yellow resinous dots are seen on both the upper and lower surfaces.

Bark: Light gray or brown, smooth.

Flowers: Dioecious, greenish yellow, in short catkins in the leaf axils from spring into summer.

Fruits: Rounded, with a blue-gray coating, to 1 cm in diameter, held along the branches of female plants from fall into winter.

Habitat: Probably most common in hammock and swamp edges with full sun, but may also grow in drier habitats such as pinelands; it tends to form thickets.

Growth Form: Shrub to small tree.

Key Features: The narrow, toothed leaves combined with the small blue-gray fruits will identify Southern Bayberry.

Comments: Southern Bayberry is found throughout Florida, including the Keys; the fruits yield wax to make scented candles and are relished by many birds for their high fat content. Although not a legume, the roots fix atmospheric nitrogen in the soil.

Marlberry
Ardisia escallonioides

Plant Family: Myrsinaceae
Leaves: Alternate, simple, shiny, elliptic to obovate, to 15 cm, appearing clustered at the twig ends, the leaf margins often reflex up and the midrib is depressed.
Bark: Light gray, smooth; the twig ends that lack flowers or fruits end in a brown stipule.
Flowers: White with yellow stamens, five petals, aromatic, in clusters near the branch ends throughout the year.
Fruits: Green drupes that ripen to shiny black, to 1 cm, found in clusters near the branch ends any time of year; edible, eaten by birds and small mammals.
Habitat: Marlberry is common in the understory of hammocks and pinelands.
Growth Form: Shrub to small tree.

Similar Species: Myrsine *(Myrsine cubana)* has green stipules at the twig ends and the flowers and fruits are held back along the branches. Coral Ardisia *(Ardisia crenata)* is a non-native landscape plant that has become invasive in hammocks; its leaves have rounded teeth and the ripe fruits are red.
Comments: The range of Marlberry includes south Florida, the West Indies, Mexico and Central America.

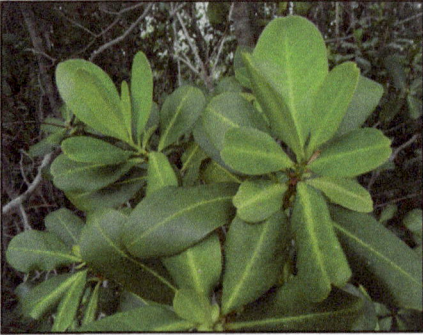

Myrsine
Myrsine cubana

Plant Family: Myrsinaceae

Leaves: Alternate, simple, obovate, lustrous, to 10 cm, appearing whorled at the twig ends, apices may be notched; new leaves, if present, are smaller and bright green.

Bark: Light brown to gray, twigs end in a green stipule.

Flowers: Creamy yellow, small, found along the leafless parts of the branches in winter.

Fruits: Green drupes that ripen to blue-black, to about 1 cm, held along the leafless parts of the branches where they may persist for much of the year.

Habitat: Common in hammocks and pinelands.

Growth Form: Shrub to small tree.

Similar Species: Marlberry *(Ardisia escallonioides)* has brown stipules at the twig ends and the flowers and fruits are in clusters near the branch ends, not back along the branches.

Comments: Older references list this species as *Rapanea guianensis* or *Myrsine floridana.* Myrsine ranges as far south as Brazil, it is at the northern limit of its range here in Florida.

Bottlebrush
Callistemon viminalis

Plant Family: Myrtaceae

Leaves: Alternate, simple, lanceolate, to 10 cm long.

Bark: Dark gray, deeply fissured.

Flowers: Individually small, with long red stamens held on narrow, pendulous clusters; all year, peaking in spring and summer.

Fruits: Brown knob-like cups in narrow clusters that hold many tiny seeds; fall, also at other times of the year.

Habitat: Planted in parks and gardens, naturalized along roadways and other disturbed sites in south Florida.

Growth Form: Small shrubby tree with attractive weeping branches.

Key Features: The weeping growth form and profuse red flowers will identify Bottlebrush.

Comments: Bottlebrush is native to Australia; it is also grown as an ornamental in Arizona and southern California. The former scientific name was *Melaleuca viminalis*.

Melaleuca
(Cajeput)
Melaleuca quinquenervia

Plant Family: Myrtaceae

Leaves: Alternate, simple, elliptic, to 10 cm, the veins run parallel to the leaf margins.

Bark: Whitish, peeling off in large, loose flakes; the inner bark is reddish-brown.

Flowers: Small, white, with bushy stamens, in bottle-brushed shaped clusters at the ends of the branches; present at any time of year, peaking in winter.

Fruits: Small, sessile, woody capsules in clusters on the branches; each capsule contains hundreds of tiny seeds.

Habitat: Most common on wet disturbed sites, such as along roadsides and canal banks, it also occurs in pinelands, marshes, cypress swamps and sawgrass prairies.

Growth Form: Small to medium-sized fast-growing tree, often in dense single species stands (as shown).

Key Feature: The whitish peeling bark will identify this weedy tree.

Comments: Melaleuca is native to Australia and New Guinea; it is one of the most problematic invasive species in south Florida, covering thousands of acres, including large areas of the Everglades. Recent biological control efforts using insects have had some success.

Bahama Maiden Bush
Heterosavia bahamensis

Plant Family: Phyllanthaceae
Leaves: Alternate, simple, stiff, shiny, elliptic to obovate, apices blunt-pointed, rounded, or notched, to about 6 cm long, the midrib is noticeably yellow. Paired brown stipules may be present at the base of the petioles.

Bark: Light gray or brown, rough, with many lenticels.

Flowers: Monoecious, greenish yellow, small, in the leaf axils; appearing from spring into early summer.

Fruits: A globular, green, three-lobed capsule, ripening to brown, to 1 cm, held singly on short stalks in the leaf axils from summer into fall.

Habitat: Sandy soils and coastal scrub of the Lower Keys, listed as endangered in Florida.

Growth Form: Shrub to small tree.

Key Features: The Lower Keys habitat, elliptic to obovate leaves with yellow midribs, and distinctive fruits will identify Bahama Maiden Bush.

Comments: Bahama Maiden Bush is more common on the Bahamas and the islands of the Caribbean; the pictured specimen was photographed on Big Pine Key. It was formerly classified as *Savia bahamensis*.

Sea Grape
Coccoloba uvifera

Plant Family: Polygonaceae

Leaves: Alternate, simple, round, to 25 cm, the central vein is red at the base; new leaves have an attractive bronze color, which soon turns green and finally red with age; the leaf petioles clasp the stem.

Bark: Light gray, smooth.

Flowers: Dioecious, green to white, in long pendulous racemes that are seen throughout the year, peaking in spring and summer.

Fruits: Green, ripening to red-purple, to 2.5 cm in diameter, in long clusters on the female tree, edible. They may be eaten raw, used to make jellies and jams, or fermented to make wine.

Habitat: Coastal hammocks, beaches; also widely planted; Sea Grape is drought-hardy and salt-tolerant.

Growth Form: Small to medium-sized tree.

Similar Species: Sea Grape is related to Pigeon Plum (*Coccoloba diversifolia*), however, the large, rounded leaves of Sea Grape are unmistakable. Both *Coccoloba* species share the characteristic that the leaf petiole clasps the stem.

Comments: Sea Grape is a Florida and West Indies native that has been introduced as a coastal tree to Mexico, Central and South America, Hawaii, and several countries in the tropical Pacific for its attractive foliage and useful fruits.

Pigeon Plum
Coccoloba diversifolia

Plant Family: Polygonaceae

Leaves: Alternate, simple, leathery, elliptic to oval, to 10 cm on mature trees, but young shoots may have much longer and larger leaves (as compared); the leaf petioles clasp the stem.

Bark: Gray to brown, scaly, the trunk on mature specimens has a muscular appearance.

Flowers: Dioecious, white, in racemes in the leaf axils from spring into summer.

Fruits: Rounded, green, ripening to dark red, to 1 cm in diameter, held in racemes on the female plant from summer into fall; relished by birds.

Habitat: Hammocks

Growth Form: Small to medium-sized tree.

Similar Species: Pigeon Plum is related to Sea Grape *(Coccoloba uvifera)*, but the large round leaves of that tree are unmistakable.

Comments: Pigeon Plum is one of south Florida's more common hammock trees; learn to recognize it by the leaf petioles that clasp the stem and the elliptic to oval leathery leaves that vary greatly in size (hence the specific name).

Milkbark
Drypetes diversifolia

Plant Family: Putranjivaceae

Leaves: Alternate, simple, dark green, leathery, oval to broadly elliptic, to 12 cm, petioles and midribs are yellowish; the leaves are found in a flat two-ranked arrangement on the twigs and branches. The leaves on young saplings may look quite different – they are holly-like, with spiky margins, presumably a defense against herbivores.

Bark: Whitish, rough, with blotches of lichens.

Flowers: Dioecious, greenish white, in very small clusters in the leaf axils; appearing from late spring to early summer, sometimes at other times of the year.

Fruits: A white drupe to 2 cm in diameter; typically seen from fall into winter.

Habitat: Hammocks of the Keys.

Growth Form: Small to medium-sized tree.

Similar Species: Guiana-plum *(Drypetes lateriflora)*, of the same genus, has light brown bark, red fruits, and narrower leaves.

Comments: Milkbark is listed as an endangered species that is found only within Keys hammocks.

Guiana-plum
Drypetes lateriflora

Plant Family: Putranjivaceae
Leaves: Alternate, simple, elliptic, leathery, apices pointed, to 10 cm, the terminal leaves are smaller than leaves further back on the branches.
Bark: Light brown to gray, smooth on young trees, rougher on older trees.
Flowers: Dioecious, greenish white, in small clusters in the leaf axils from late winter to spring.
Fruits: A red, downy drupe, to 1 cm in diameter, held in short clusters on the female plant; present in the early summer.
Habitat: Atlantic coastal and Keys hammocks.
Growth Form: Small tree.
Similar Species: Milkbark *(Drypetes diversifolia)*, of the same genus, has whiter bark and white fruits.
Comments: Guiana-plum is somewhat more common than Milkbark, ranging north from the Keys onto the peninsula, but is listed as a threatened species in Florida.

Coffee Colubrina
(Snakebark)
Colubrina arborescens

Plant Family: Rhamnaceae
Leaves: Alternate, simple, stiff, ovate, to 15 cm, dark green above with reddish brown hairs below, especially along the veins. New leaves and twigs are reddish brown.
Bark: Light gray and flaking off like a snake sheds its skin.
Flowers: Yellow, with 5 petals, in axillary clusters in the summer.
Fruits: A round, green, 3-part capsule that turns blue-black, to 1 cm, held in short clusters near the branch ends from fall into winter; when ripe they open abruptly, catapulting the seeds some distance from the parent.
Habitat: Hammocks of the Keys and the Lower Peninsula.
Growth Form: Shrub to small tree.
Similar Species: Soldierwood *(Colubrina elliptica)* has thin leaves with orange fruits; Cuban Colubrina *(Colubrina cubensis)* also has leathery leaves but with round-toothed margins.
Comments: Coffee Colubrina is listed as an endangered species in Florida where it reaches the northern part of its range. It also inhabits the West Indies, Mexico, and Central and South America.

Soldierwood
Colubrina elliptica

Plant Family: Rhamnaceae
Leaves: Alternate, simple, thin, ovate to elliptic, apices long pointed, to 10 cm. Two small glands can be seen on the basal leaf margin.
Bark: Light reddish gray.
Flowers: Yellow, with 5 petals, in axillary clusters in summer.
Fruits: A round, green, 3-part capsule that turns orange, to 1 cm; seen fall to winter.
Habitat: Hammock edges of the Everglades and the Keys.
Growth Form: Shrub to small tree.
Similar Species: Coffee Colubrina *(Colubrina arborescens)* has leathery leaves with dark fruits; Cuban Colubrina *(Colubrina cubensis)* also has leathery leaves but with round-toothed margins.

Comments: The common name refers to the popping sound made by the ripe fruits when abruptly releasing their seeds, sending them a distance from the parent tree. The bark is used in the West Indies to produce Mauby (also spelled Mavi) a popular drink. Soldierwood is listed as an endangered species in Florida.

143

West Indies Cherry
Prunus myrtifolia

Plant Family: Rosaceae

Leaves: Alternate, simple, ovate to elliptic, with wavy margins and a pointed drip tip, to 12 cm; glossy green above, light green below; new growth is reddish; the crushed leaves have a fruity scent.

Bark: Gray to brown, smooth on younger trees, becoming rougher on older trees.

Flowers: Small, white, with 5 petals and obviously long stamens, held in profuse linear clusters in the leaf axils from late fall into winter.

Fruits: A dark orange drupe, to 1 cm in diameter, in short clusters in the leaf axils, the pulp is edible but not very palatable; usually seen spring to early summer.

Habitat: Rockland hammocks of Miami-Dade County, where it is not common.

Growth Form: Small to medium-sized tree.

Key Feature: The fruity odor of the crushed leaves (some liken it to bitter almond), will identify West Indies Cherry.

Comments: West Indies Cherry is listed as a threatened species in south Florida. Both the leaves and the seeds are toxic if ingested.

Carolina Willow
(Coastal Plain Willow)
Salix caroliniana

Plant Family: Salicaceae

Leaves: Alternate, simple, lanceolate, to 15 cm, often lightly toothed, green above and lighter beneath.

Bark: Light gray to brown, rough and blocky on older specimens.

Flowers: Dioecious, the yellow flowers appear along the branches in short catkins from late winter into spring.

Fruits: Small two-part capsules, each containing many tiny hairy seeds that are released to the air to float to new habitat. The white-tufted fruits appear after the flowers in the spring and summer.

Habitat: Like most other Salix species, Carolina Willow is found near water or in moist soil and is common in the south Florida peninsula; it is uncommon on the Keys.

Growth Form: Small tree.

Similar Species: The leaves are similar to Black Willow *(Salix nigra)*, but that species is limited to northern Florida.

Comments: The leaf buds press closely to the twigs and have a single scale, which is characteristic of all the willows.

Varnish Leaf
(Florida Hop Bush)
Dodonaea viscosa

Plant Family: Sapindaceae

Leaves: Alternate, simple, oblan-ceolate, shiny, to 12 cm, surface somewhat sticky like wet varnish.

Bark: Brown, fissured, shaggy on older trees.

Flowers: Greenish yellow, in sparse clusters at the twig ends; appearing from late fall to early spring.

Fruits: An angular hop-like cap-sule that is yellow-green and red, to 2.5 cm, quite noticeable in the spring to early summer.

Habitat: The understory and edges of pinelands and hammocks, sandy soils.

Growth Form: Shrub to small tree.

Key Features: The narrow, shiny, sticky leaves, and hop-like fruits, will identify Varnish Leaf.

Comments: Most of the species in the genus *Dodonaea* are found in Australia, however, Varnish Leaf has a worldwide distribution in warmer regions of Australia, Asia, Africa, and the Americas. In the United States it is found in Florida, Arizona, Califor-nia, and Hawaii.

Satin Leaf
Chrysophyllum oliviforme

Plant Family: Sapotaceae
Leaves: Alternate, simple, stiff, to 10 cm, oval to broadly elliptic, apices pointed or rounded, top surface shiny dark green, bottom surface distinctly coppery, smooth, and finely hairy, soft like satin.
Bark: Gray-brown, fissured and flaky, the trunk is normally straight, not shrubby; the twigs are orange-brown.
Flowers: Small, pale yellow, bell-shaped, with five petals, in short clusters in the leaf axils; present any time of the year.
Fruits: A green berry that ripens to brown or black and is shaped like an olive (hence the specific name), to 2.5 cm, edible; seen throughout the year.
Habitat: The understory of hammocks and pinelands, mature specimens may reach canopy height; it is listed as threatened in the wild in Florida, but is widely planted for its attractive leaves.
Growth Form: Small to medium-sized tree.
Key Feature: The leaves of Satin Leaf are unmistakable.
Comments: Satin Leaf is related to Caimito *(Chrysophyllum cainito)*, a West Indian tree that is cultivated for its larger and edible fruits.

Wild Dilly
Manilkara jaimiqui

Plant Family: Sapotaceae
Leaves: Alternate, simple, stiff, oblong to elliptic, to 10 cm, top surface dull green, bottom surface with reddish-brown hairs; apices rounded or notched; broken leaves reveal a milky sap. The leaves cluster at the twig ends.
Bark: Dark gray, blocky on older trees.
Flowers: Small, yellow, with 6 petals, on stalks clustered in the leaf axils; spring to summer, sometimes at other times of the year.
Fruits: A light brown rounded berry, to 4 cm in diameter; typically summer to fall.
Habitat: The edges of coastal hammocks, more common on the Keys; salt tolerant.
Growth Form: Small tree.
Similar Species: Wild Dilly is related to Sapodilla *(Manilkara zapota)* and the leaves are similar, however, Sapodilla has larger fruits.
Comments: Other current references call this species *Manilkara bahamensis.* Wild Dilly is listed as a threatened species in Florida.

Sapodilla
Manilkara zapota

Plant Family: Sapotaceae

Leaves: Alternate, simple, glossy, narrowly elliptic, margins wavy, to 12 cm; they tend to cluster at the branch ends.

Bark: Medium gray to brown, smooth on young trees, rougher on older specimens.

Flowers: Monoecious, white, small, long-stalked, with six petals; all year.

Fruits: Spherical to egg-shaped, light brown, up to 10 cm long; late spring to fall in Florida, peaking in mid-summer. When ripe the flesh is edible and very sweet, resembling that of a pear.

Habitat: Sapodilla is known to naturalize along hammock margins and on disturbed sites.

Growth Form: Potentially a large tree; cultivated trees are usually smaller.

Similar Species: The related Wild Dilly has similar leaves but smaller fruits.

Comments: Sapodilla is native to southern Mexico and Central America; the specific name is derived from the Aztec word for the tree. It is cultivated in Florida, the West Indies, and several countries in the Old World tropics, including India. Plant breeders have developed a surprisingly large number of cultivars of this commercially important tree.

149

Monkey's Apple
Mimusops coriacea

Plant Family: Sapotaceae

Leaves: Alternate, simple, thick and leathery, obovate, the apices are often notched, to 20 cm; tend to cluster toward the branch ends.

Bark: Brown, smooth on young trees, fissured on older specimens.

Flowers: Yellow-white, found singly or in clusters in the leaf axils from summer into fall.

Fruits: A green berry, ripening to yellow, up to 6 cm in diameter, with 2 to 4 dark seeds. The pulp is edible, but is rather sticky and mealy, not recommended.

Habitat: Mostly cultivated sites on the east coast and although not common in wild habitats it may sometimes naturalize. It is not considered invasive at this time. There is a large, attractive specimen close to the visitor center at Fairchild Tropical Botanic Garden.

Growth Form: Medium-sized to large tree.

Similar Species: Autograph Tree (*Clusia rosea*) has very similar leaves, but they are opposite along the stems.

Comments: Monkey's Apple is native to Madagascar and the Mascarenes, islands east of Madagascar in the Indian Ocean.

Saffron Plum
Sideroxylon celastrinum

Plant Family: Sapotaceae
Leaves: Alternate, simple, obovate, leathery, green above, paler beneath, to 4 cm, clustered on spur twigs; short spines may be present at the twig bases and larger thorns appear along the branches.
Bark: Dark brown-gray, smoother on young trees, fissured to blocky on mature trees.
Flowers: Small, white, fragrant, in clusters in the leaf axils; spring to summer, also at other times of the year.

Fruits: A green stalked berry to 2.5 cm that ripens to blue-black, edible; late summer into winter. The fruits are eaten by wildlife.
Habitat: Hammocks on the coast.
Growth Form: Small tree.
Similar Species: Tough Bully *(Sideroxylon tenax)* has leaves densely brown hairy beneath. Florida Bully *(Sideroxylon reclinatum)* has smaller fruits and prefers pinelands and drier soils rather than coastal hammocks.
Comments: The Florida species formerly assigned to the genus *Bumelia* have been moved to the genus *Sideroxylon.* Saffron Plum is called *Bumelia celastrina* in older references.

Mastic
Sideroxylon foetidissimum

Plant Family: Sapotaceae

Leaves: Alternate, simple, light green, elliptic, with yellow mid-ribs, to 20 cm; the veins are more prominent on young specimens, are less prominent with distinctive wavy edges on older trees (both are shown).

Bark: Brown and lightly rough on younger trees, light gray to brown, rough and flaking on older trees, the twigs are light brown.

Flowers: Greenish-yellow, in short, dense clusters on the twigs beneath the younger leaves; spring to summer.

Fruits: Yellow, ripening to orange, rounded, to 2.5 cm, held on the twigs beneath the younger leaves, edible; summer to fall.

Habitat: Coastal hammocks.

Growth Form: Small to large tree.

Key Features: Potentially confused with other alternate leaved hammock species, however, the combination of light gray-brown bark and wavy edged leaves held on brown twigs should identify Mastic.

Comments: In older field guides this species is called *Mastichodendron foetidissimum*.

Willow Bustic
Sideroxylon salicifolium

Plant Family: Sapotaceae

Leaves: Alternate, simple, elliptic to lanceolate, to 12 cm; narrow and willow-like.

Bark: Brown, lightly fissured, with reddish inner bark, smoother on young trees.

Flowers: Monoecious, white, tiny, with five petals, in clusters on the branches below the new leaves, quite fragrant; seen late winter to early summer.

Fruits: A green, elliptic berry, ripening to black, to 1 cm, held on short stalks in clusters on the older parts of the branches; they are eaten by several bird species.

Habitat: Hammocks and pinelands.

Growth Form: Small to medium-sized tree.

Similar Species: The densely clustered flowers and fruits distinguish Willow Bustic from the true Willows (*Salix* spp.)

Comments: Willow Bustic has been re-assigned by taxonomists to the genus *Sideroxylon*. In older volumes this species is referenced as *Dipholis salicifolia*.

Potato Tree
Solanum erianthum

Plant Family: Solanaceae

Leaves: Alternate, simple, light green, narrowly elliptic, large, up to 30 cm long, soft and downy to the touch; the apices may be rounded or pointed.

Bark: Light brown, hairy, the branches are covered with large leaf scars.

Flowers: White with 5 petals, stamens yellow, held in flat-topped clusters at the branch ends at any time of year.

Fruits: A green stalked berry that ripens to yellow, to 2 cm in diameter, covered with fine hairs; potentially all year, peaking in the fall.

Habitat: Open hammock edges, roadsides, field edges, disturbed sites; it is considered a pioneer species.

Growth Form: Shrub to small tree.

Key Feature: Not likely to be confused with other species, the large, light green, soft velvety leaves are the best field mark.

Comments: Potato Tree is a West Indian species that has been introduced into other tropical countries for the medicinal uses of the leaves, which may be taken internally as a tea or applied to the skin as a poultice. Potato Tree is in the same plant family as the garden potato.

Bay Cedar
Suriana maritima

Plant Family: Surianaceae
Leaves: Alternate, simple, linear, narrow, to 5 cm, somewhat fleshy, densely crowded at the tips of the branches; the crushed leaves have a cedar-like aroma.
Bark: Reddish brown, rough.
Flowers: Yellow, small, yet quite attractive, with five petals, found nestled within the leaves at the branch ends; usually winter to spring, but also at other times of the year.
Fruits: Brown nutlets, less than 1 cm in diameter.
Habitat: Beaches and sandy coastal thickets, it is not found inland; highly salt-resistant and drought-tolerant.
Growth Form: Shrub to small tree.
Key Features: The beach or sandy habitat combined with the small linear leaves strongly clustered at the branch ends are diagnostic characteristics, separating Bay Cedar from all other south Florida trees.
Comments: Like the Coconut Palm, the seeds of Bay Cedar (although very much smaller) can germinate on distant beaches after spending long periods in saltwater, resulting in a worldwide distribution on tropical coasts.

Joewood
Jacquinia keyensis

Plant Family: Theophrastaceae

Leaves: Alternate, simple, oblanceolate, thick and shiny, to 5 cm, the margins may roll under, the apices may be rounded or notched.

Bark: Light mottled gray, smooth, usually with lichens present, the branches have a crooked appearance.

Flowers: White to cream colored, small, with five petals, in short clusters at the branch ends, quite fragrant; appearing summer into fall.

Fruits: A stalked, rounded, green-yellow berry that ripens to reddish orange, to 1 cm; from fall into winter.

Habitat: Coastal thickets of the Keys and also Sanibel Island; not found in other counties of south Florida.

Growth Form: Shrub to small tree.

Key Features: Small thick leaves, crooked branches, and stalked green fruits that turn reddish orange will identify Joewood.

Comments: Joewood is listed as a threatened species in Florida.

Tallowwood
(Hog Plum)
Ximenia americana

Plant Family: Ximeniaceae
Leaves: Alternate, simple, oblong to elliptic, to 8 cm long, margins reflexed up from the mid-rib, apices rounded or notched, sharp spines in the leaf axils; spur branches may be present; the crushed leaves have an almond odor.
Bark: Brown to gray, smooth to fissured.
Flowers: Small, yellow-white, with 4 petals, held on long stalks; throughout the year, peaking in the late spring.

Fruits: A rounded green drupe to about 3 cm in diameter, ripening to yellow-orange; edible. Reportedly eaten by gopher tortoises and other wildlife for the high energy content.
Habitat: Dry hammocks, thickets, pinelands, and sand pine scrub.
Growth Form: Shrub to small tree.
Similar Species: Distinguished from thorny plants in the genus *Sideroxylon*, such as Saffron Plum, by the relatively large yellow-orange fruits.

Comments: Tallowwood has a remarkably broad global and tropical distribution - it is found in Africa, Asia, Australia, and the Americas! Indigenous people use the plant for both food and medicine.

157

GLOSSARY

Alternate leaf – One leaf grows from each node of the stem.

Apex – The tip of a leaf (apices is the plural form).

Axil - The angle between a stem or twig and an attached leaf.

Base (basal) - The bottom of a tree or a leaf.

Berry – A fleshy fruit in which the seeds are embedded (example – the Stoppers).

Catkin – A spike of flowers that may be upright or hang from the twig (example - Oaks).

Compound leaf – A hardwood leaf with smaller leaflets that share a common axis from the rachis (pinnate) or that share a common point of origin (palmate).

Once-compound leaf – Single leaflets grow from the rachis.

Twice-compound leaf – Double leaflets grow from the rachis.

Crownshaft – A green cylinder of leaf bases at the top of the trunk in some palms (examples – Royal Palm, Manila Palm).

Cultivars – Different forms of the same species that have been developed by plant breeders, often focusing on the flowers or fruits (examples – Avocado, Mango, and many others).

Dioecious – Meaning two houses – when a species has male and female flowers held on separate trees (i.e., trees are either male or female; see Monoecious).

Drupe – A fruit with a fleshy outer portion and a hard inner portion that holds the seed(s) (example – Tallowwood).

Epiphyte – A plant that grows on the branches or bark of another plant but is not a parasite (example – Spanish Moss growing on Live Oak).

Elliptic – Describing a leaf that is widest in the middle and pointed at both ends, shaped like a football in outline.

Invasive species – A plant (or animal) species that is not native, but has become established in a particular habitat, and tends to out-compete native species, often to a great degree (Melaleuca, Australian Pine, and Brazilian Pepper are examples).

Fissured – A description of bark that is characterized by raised vertical ridges alternating with depressions.

Lanceolate – A leaf shaped like a lance, narrow, wider at the base and pointed toward the apex (see oblanceolate).

Leaflets – The several blades of a once-compound or twice-compound hardwood leaf.

Leaf scars – Marks on the twigs and branches of a hardwood where a leaf was formerly attached.

Lenticel – A marked pore for gas exchange; usually on narrow trunks and branches.

Midrib – The middle vein of a leaf.

Monoecious – Meaning one house – when a tree species has flowers with male and female parts on the same tree (see Dioecious).

Naturalized – Said of a cultivated or non-native plant that becomes established in the wild without human help.

Nut – A dry, single-seeded fruit, consisting of a kernel within a woody shell (example – Oaks).

Oblanceolate – A leaf shaped like a lance, but narrower toward the base and wider toward the apex (see lanceolate).

Oblong – A leaf longer than broad, with the two longer margins parallel - similar to a rectangle - but with a rounded base and apex.

Obovate – A leaf that has its widest portion towards the pointed apex (see ovate).

Opposite leaves – Two leaves grow from each node of the stem.

Oval – A leaf that is widest in the middle, with a rounded base and apex.

Ovate - A leaf that has its widest portion towards the base and has a pointed apex (see obovate).

Palmate leaf – A compound leaf in which the leaflets share a common central point of origin, as in fingers projecting from a palm.

Petal – Usually the leaf-like colored part of a flower; some flowers lack petals.

Petiole – The stem of a leaf that attaches it to the twig.

Pinnate leaf - A compound leaf in which the leaflets originate from a central axis (rachis), feather-like.

Pistil – The female part of a flower that produces the seeds.

Prickles – Short, sharp projections that grow from the epidermis of a plant.

Prop roots – Aerial roots that arch out from the main trunk and act to provide extra stability to the tree (example – Red Mangrove).

Prostrate – Lying flat on the ground – used to describe the trunk of a tree (examples include Saw Palmetto and Buttonwood).

Rachis – The central axis of a pinnate compound leaf.

Ring scars – Obvious marks on the trunk of a palm where a leaf was formerly attached.

Segment – Referring to the leaflets of a palm.

Sessile – Describes flowers and fruits attached directly to the branch, without a stalk.

Simple leaf – A leaf with a single blade.

Spines – Sharp projections in the leaf axils that are derived from stipules.

Spur twigs – Short twigs held at a 90-degree angle from a branch that often end in a point and typically have strongly clustered leaves (see Saffron Plum as an example).

Stamen – The male part of a flower that produces pollen.

Stipule – A tiny leaf located where the leaf petiole meets the stem.

Terminal – At the very end of a twig or branch.

Thorns – Sharp twigs, usually held at right angles to the stem.

Whorled leaves – More than two leaves grow from each node of the stem, typically three or four leaves at each node (see Buttonbush as an example).

Selected References

Books

Austin, Daniel F. 1995. *A Field Guide to the Plants of South Florida's Pine Rockland Community*. Dade County Department of Environmental Resources Management.

Brockman, C. Frank. 2002. *Trees of North America*. New York: St. Martin's Press.

Craighead, Frank C., 1971. *The Trees of South Florida, Volume I. The Natural Environments and Their Succession*. University of Miami Press.

Nellis, David W. 1994. *Seashore Plants of South Florida and the Caribbean: A Guide to Knowing and Growing Drought and Salt-Tolerant Plants*. Sarasota, FL: Pineapple Press.

Nelson, Gil. 1996. *The Shrubs and Woody Vines of Florida*. Sarasota, FL: Pineapple Press.

Nelson, Gil. 2011. *The Trees of Florida: A Reference and Field Guide*. Sarasota, FL: Pineapple Press.

Nelson, Gil. 2011. *Botanical Keys to Florida's Trees, Shrubs, and Woody Vines: A Guide to Field Identification*. Sarasota, FL: Pineapple Press.

Petrides, George A. 1998. *A Field Guide to Eastern Trees*. Boston: Houghton Mifflin Company.

Stevenson, George B. 1996. *Palms of South Florida*. Gainesville, FL: University Press of Florida.

Stevenson, George B. 1979. *Trees of Everglades National Park and the Florida Keys*. Miami: Banyan Books, Inc.

Tomlinson, P.B. 1980. *The Biology of Trees Native to Tropical Florida*. Allston, MA: Harvard University Printing Office.

Websites

AgroForestryTree Database.
http://www.worldagroforestrycentre.org

Atlas of Florida Vascular Plants. Institute for Systematic Botany.
http://florida.plantatlas.usf.edu

Center for Aquatic and Invasive Plants; University of Florida.
http://plants.ifas.ufl.edu

Flora of North America.
http://www.efloras.org

Florida Exotic Pest Plant Council.
http://www.fleppc.org

Florida Interactive Native Plant and Tree Distribution Range Maps.
http://www.plantmaps.com/florida-native-plants-and-trees-maps.php

Guide to Florida Plant Life.
http://www.floridaplants.com/reprintnativepls.html

Natives for Your Neighborhood. Institute for Regional Conservation.
http://regionalconservation.org

Oaks of the World.
http://oaks.of.the.world.free.fr/index.htm

Pine Rocklands.
http://www.fws.gov/southeast/vbpdfs/common/pv.pdf

Smithsonian Marine Station at Fort Pierce.
http://www.sms.si.edu

United States Department of Agriculture. Plants Database.
http://plants.usda.gov

United States Forest Service
http://www.fs.fed.us

University of Florida, IFAS Extension
http://lee.ifas.ufl.edu/Hort/GardenPubsAZ

INDEX TO SCIENTIFIC NAMES

INDEX TO COMMON NAMES

www.ingramcontent.com/pod-product-compliance
Lightning Source LLC
Chambersburg PA
CBHW041257040426
42334CB00028BA/3051